KEEPING LIFE IN PERSPECTIVE

© 1996 by Jim Henry
All rights reserved

Published by Broadman & Holman Publishers, Nashville, Tennessee
Acquisitions & Development Editor: Janis Whipple
Interior Design: Leslie Joslin
Printed in the United States of America

4261-96
0-8054-6196-5

Dewey Decimal Classification: 248.84
Subject Heading: CHRISTIAN LIFE
Library of Congress Card Catalog Number: 96-17179

Unless otherwise noted, Scripture quotations are from the Holy
Bible, New International Version, copyright © 1973, 1978, 1984 by
International Bible Society.

Library of Congress Cataloging-in-Publication Data
Henry, Jim, 1937- .
Keeping life in perspective : sharpening your sense of what's
    important / Jim Henry with Marilyn Jeffcoat
        p.   cm.
ISBN 0-8054-6196-5 (hardcover)
1. Christian life—Baptist authors. 2. Henry, Jim, 1937- .
    I. Title.   II. Jeffcoat, Marilyn.
    BV4501.2.H3743   1996
    248.4—dc20

    96-17179
    CIP

96 97 98 99 00 5 4 3 2 1

KEEPING LIFE IN PERSPECTIVE

Sharpening Your Sense of What's Important

JIM HENRY

WITH MARILYN JEFFCOAT

BROADMAN & HOLMAN PUBLISHERS

Nashville, Tennessee

This book is dedicated with love and gratitude in memory of my deceased dad, James William Henry, and mother-in-law, Bertha Mae Sturgeon; and to my beloved mother, Kathryn Fisher Henry, and father-in-law, Samuel L. Sturgeon. Each in their own way were used by God's Holy Spirit to flesh out eternal principles that assisted me in keeping life in perspective.

CONTENTS

ACKNOWLEDGMENTS

Putting together a book is getting to be more complicated than filling out an income tax return! This effort would have never been realized without the research, writing, editing, and bulldog determination of Marilyn Jeffcoat; the research of Walter Walker; the patience, diligence, and efficiency of my assistant, Sandi Mathis; the understanding of our great staff and the fellowship of First Baptist Church, Orlando, whose encouragement, prayers, and extra effort enabled me to serve as their pastor and the president of the Southern Baptist Convention; and my wife, Jeanette, whose wisdom, counsel, and memories have been an encyclopedic resource from which to draw.

FOREWORD

Like a kaleidoscope, ever changing, ever new; like a mariner glancing from star to star, searching in vain for the North Star; like a compass spinning wildly at the Poles; . . . modern life for believer and unbeliever alike is often a whirling dervish of new plans, direction changes, and uncertainty The mad dashes to redetermine the priorities of each day—the endless race to sharpen perspectives and distinguish between the good and the best, the important and the urgent—are the mine fields through which we precariously step day by day. As desperate as is the plight, however, even greater is the need to drive the stakes, build the foundation, establish the parameters, and move with grace and confidence through life. Priorities and perspectives: they're what shape us, determine everything about us, and are the crucial make-or-break for the life of every human being on planet earth.

Jim Henry writes a great book because Jim Henry is a great man. What he writes, he is. He's got it together, so he can tell us how. He's made the journey with style and grace, and the gracious president of the world's largest Protestant denomination has done us a great service in his wake-up call to set our priorities in order and live life with eternal perspectives. The whole book is rich with biblical examples and contemporary illustrations into which you can sink your teeth. It may be the most classical exposition you will ever read on life and Matthew 6:33, "Seek ye first the kingdom of God, and his righteousness, and all these things shall be added unto you." That's the priority that lends a perspective that makes it all come together. Happy reading!

Dr. John R. Bisagno, Pastor
First Baptist Church, Houston, Texas

CHAPTER ONE

DEFINING OUR PERSPECTIVE

I stopped what I was doing when I passed the television and saw the footage from an airplane crash. As the camera panned the site, there were images of suitcases, shoes, stuffed animals, and other personal possessions—poignant reminders these were real people who lost their lives in that fatal crash.

When the jumbo jet hit the ground, the tail section broke off and threw one row of seats from the fuselage. While the main body of the plane turned into a cartwheeling fireball, this row of seats miraculously came to rest in an upright position with its two passengers still strapped in, terrified but relatively unharmed! The televised report told of these two survivors unbuckling their seat belts and walking away from the crash. When interviewed, one of them commented, "This experience has made me stop and reconsider what really matters in my life."

I thought to myself, *I bet that changed your perspective!* God in His sovereign plan, while allowing the lives of the other passengers to be cut short, gave this man a miraculous extension to his days—a new lease on life. I couldn't help but wonder how his life changed that day. How did this amazing experience color the way he looked at his family, his work, his leisure, his concerns, and, most importantly, his relationship to God? Do you think God got his attention that day?

1

WHAT MATTERS

"What's it going to take to get your attention?" the irate mother loudly asked her obviously uncomfortable teenage son as they entered the church. She was shaking what looked like a report card as she inquired, "Is it going to take a truckload of bricks falling from the sky on your head to get you to open your eyes and see what you are doing with your life?" I guess she didn't know her pastor was walking behind them as she grilled her son. It was one of those times when not speaking was in order, so as not to embarrass the mother or mortify the son.

This sound byte left the impression of an obviously upset mother and her desire to see a change in her son's perspective. Casual observation suggested there were some things going on in his life which were distracting him from doing his best in school. His friends, perhaps? His social life? A girlfriend? Pressures at school? Pressures at home? Whatever the distractions were, this young man needed to change his focus to get his mom off his back.

What does it take to get your attention and shape your perspective of the important things in life? A traumatic experience like the plane crash? The rebuke of an irate parent? Loss of a job? Divorce? Terminal illness? God can effectively work in and through, above and beyond, all means to bring us to an acknowledgment of our need for change in the way we look at life and in our relationship to Him.

I once pastored a young mother of four who was forced to assume the sole responsibility of raising her children in the faith. Without her husband's help, she got her children up, dressed, fed, and to church every Sunday morning, week in and week out. Her husband, Red, was a hard-driving labor union leader who had little interest in spiritual matters. As much as the wife prayed and as hard as she tried, she could not get her husband to see his need for the Lord or his need to help raise his children to believe in the Lord. Burdened for her husband, she asked that I come by their home and talk with him.

Somewhat reluctantly I came to their house, rang the doorbell, and then prayed no one would be at home! I had read about this guy in the newspapers and knew of his reputation for toughness in dealing with people. I was not, to say the least, enthusiastic about the prospect of eyeballing him about his need for Christ.

As God would have it, someone was at home. The door opened and, to my chagrin, this tough guy cordially invited me in. After exchanging pleasantries, I began to share the gospel with him. Surprisingly, he seemed to listen intently. I was feeling pretty good about this visit until he said, "Brother Jim, I don't have time right now for the Lord. I'm just not interested, but thank you for taking the time to come by today. I will think about it later." With that curt response, I prayed with him and left.

Several months later, I was abruptly awakened around midnight. It was a telephone call from the director of the local funeral home. He told me that four young people from our community had been in a tragic automobile accident. Three of them were dead and the fourth, the son of the man I had visited earlier, was in critical condition. It fell upon me to go door to door, informing all the parents of the accident victims and of their immediate need to go to the hospital to check on the condition of their children. Needless to say, it was one of the saddest nights of my life.

Steve, the fourth teenager, was a young man with whom I had prayed a few years earlier when he asked to receive Jesus Christ as his personal Savior. The accident had left him in a coma. The next day I was asked by the family to go to the hospital to check on him. His dad, who'd had little time for God, met me at the door. This big, tough labor union man was now tender, broken, and tearful. I walked with him into the intensive care room and stood by his side as we looked at the broken body of his boy. He wept like a baby. All I could do was to put my arms around him, seek to console him, and pray lovingly with him. Shortly thereafter, the boy died.

This kind of tragedy can tear a family apart or leave them with a grief that forever follows them. In Red's case, it changed his life for the better. Following his son's funeral service, which I conducted, Red met me and said, "Brother Jim, I'll be in church this Sunday."

It was Easter Sunday, and Red was right where he said he would be. At the close of the service, when I gave the invitation to accept Christ, the music had barely begun before Red was in the aisle, nearly running to the front of the church! He tearfully embraced me and said, "My son is in heaven. I want to join him there one day. I accept Jesus as my Lord and Savior."

Red's baptism was a joyful experience. He boldly proclaimed his faith in Christ, saying, "Now I know I'll see my boy again! I know I'll see him one day!" Red became an active church member

3

and a loving, responsible husband. The Spirit of God changed his life, but, sadly, it took this tragedy to open his eyes.

Unfortunately, many of us must be shaken by tragedy or near-catastrophe for us to do that kind of refocusing and reevaluation. The nonstop pace of life in America certainly keeps our minds and schedules occupied. Like a hypnotist's dangling, shiny object, the constant motion of today's culture tends to dull our senses and rob us of the awareness of what is important around us.

Paul wrote to the Corinthian church, "The god of this age has blinded the minds of unbelievers, so that they cannot see the light of the gospel of the glory of Christ, who is the image of God" (2 Cor. 4:4). This is still true today. People are blinded to spiritual realities by the gods of our age—materialism, humanism, secularism, and so on. They need help to clearly see the truths of God. They need help to see what truly matters in life.

BRINGING LIFE INTO PERSPECTIVE

Scientists asked for help in seeing the heavenlies. NASA gave them Hubble! It did not, however, initially give them the perspective they wanted. A while back, a story appeared in *U.S. News & World Report* entitled "A Telescope Built by Mr. Magoo."[1] (For anyone under forty who doesn't know, Mr. Magoo was an extremely near-sighted cartoon character.) It dealt with the Hubble telescope's difficulties.

To fully appreciate the article's title, you must understand that back in 1637 René Descartes, a French mathematician, described how telescopes should be designed. He said builders should grind an optic lens to avoid blurred images caused by a phenomenon called "spherical aberrations."

In 1990, NASA launched the $1.5 billion Hubble space telescope. They proclaimed its mirrors, one of which measured ninety-four feet in diameter, were the most perfect ever made. The mirrors, however, were shaped incorrectly. Light reflecting from the edge of the mirror focused on a different plane than light from the center of the mirror. Because of the spherical aberration, the telescope had *myopia*.

Apparently the people at NASA didn't read Descartes! Hubble was near-sighted, and NASA had to subsequently fit it with multi-million dollar corrective lenses.

A near-sighted person's eyes are elongated and, consequently, distant objects are focused in front of the eye's retina, not directly on it. The person with myopia, or near-sightedness, can focus on objects which are close to him, but not on things which are far away.[2] There are many people who have this problem and need some corrective measure to see things properly.

Most of us suffer from hereditary *spiritual* myopia—that is, we easily focus on the things at hand but have a hard time focusing on the issues of life that are either far removed or do not currently represent pressing needs. The things on which we focus are often not those things which are most valuable or most meaningful. We, too, need help to see things as God would have us see them.

Are you being robbed of the blessings of life—joy, purpose, contentment, and relationships—because your perspective is out of focus? Is your worldview distorted? To a large degree, the quality of your life is determined by how clearly the light of Christ illumines the way you look at the important matters in life. Jesus said, "'The eye is the lamp of the body. If your eyes are good, your whole body will be full of light. But if your eyes are bad, your whole body will be full of darkness. If then the light within you is darkness, how great is that darkness'" (Matt. 6:22).

If our spiritual vision is poor, then we are unable to see other things in their proper light. Until He has our undivided attention, and we allow Him to correct the problem in our short-sightedness, we will never be able to view life as He created it to be. We must be committed to change our perspective—and our lifestyle.

FOXHOLE COMMITMENTS

Anyone who has lived very long has probably had a few traumatic eye-openers. People who have experienced a great awakening through crisis usually have one thing in common: it's hard for them to keep that acute sense of value and perspective once they get back into the grind of daily life. It just slips through their fingers.

Paul Azinger was the number-two all-time money winner on the PGA Tour when, in 1994, cancer was discovered in his right shoulder. After nine months of tortuous radiation and chemotherapy, he was declared "cancer free." Of course, coming face-to-face with death changed the way Paul looked at life. In an interview for *New Man Magazine,*[3] he commented on his struggle to maintain the perspective on life he gained through the events of the previous year. "Sitting at home watching golfers lose it over missing a putt, I wanted to jump through the television and remind them of all the

5

things for which they had to be thankful. I'm back in the routine now, trying to hold on to that sense of abundant gratitude. I can see how it is not like it was when I was sick. I have found that it is so easy to get back to where I was before."

Paul Azinger is committed to holding on to the perspective he gained through his illness. Not everyone who has such an eye-opening experience is as committed. Their commitments might be called "foxhole commitments." The phrase originally referred to the spiritual commitments made by men fighting in the terrible trench warfare of World War I. Tens of thousands of young men lost their lives in those trenches. Yet of those who survived, many never followed through on their commitments.

Often our inability to carry out promises and resolutions is not just a matter of our sincerity or our willpower during or after a time of crisis. It is a matter of hanging on to the keen perspective which initially prompted us to make the promises. In times of crisis, we see things clearly, but over time we don't see things with such clarity. With that loss of perspective, we become unable to honor our commitments.

When I was younger, several fellows my age came to Christ around the same time as I. One boy was a good friend of mine. He had a great sense of humor and a charismatic personality. As time went on, I noticed his spiritual vision became blurred, and, consequently, he began to stray from the commitments we had both made. He chose some friends and habits that further alienated him from the things of God.

From time to time, I would talk to my friend about his choices and he would always say, "I know I need to quit this and I know I need to do that. I'll be back in church next Sunday." And so it went.

This young man, who had been a good friend, became more and more a stranger to me. After graduation, we lost touch. Some years later, I found out my friend had begun drinking heavily and had drifted into a lifestyle that got him in trouble with the law. The last I heard he was in a penitentiary. I wonder what happened to his commitment.

Following the Parable of the Sower, Jesus gives this explanation:

"This is the meaning of the parable: The seed is the word of God. Those along the path are the ones who hear, and then the devil comes and takes away the word from their hearts, so that they cannot believe and be saved. . . . The seed that fell among thorns stands for those

6

who hear, but as they go on their way they are choked by life's worries, riches and pleasures, and they do not mature. But the seed on good soil stands for those with a noble and good heart, who hear the word, retain it, and by persevering produce a crop." (Luke 8:11–12, 14–15)

The devil delights in commitments which don't take root. He does everything within his power to rob us of the joy of commitments fulfilled. For us to make commitments that take root, we need our eyes opened by God the Holy Spirit to see that which is noble and good. With His help, we can persevere in keeping a clear perspective of who we are in Jesus Christ and what He's done—and is doing—for us. This is crucial in preventing Satan from using the dulling effect of this present world to steal the seed of illumination from our hearts.

Unforgettable Mistakes

When we don't see things clearly—as they should be seen—we can make some huge mistakes. Sellers of fake diamonds can confuse our discernment of what is truly valuable by setting cubic zirconia in precious metals, perhaps surrounded by precious or semiprecious stones. These faux diamonds may, to the naked eye, look like diamonds, but they do not hold the value of the genuine stones. It would be a costly mistake to pay for quality diamonds and receive these much less valuable substitutes.

Discernment is essential in decision making. Satan is the master deceiver and would love to convince us the selfish, humanistic beliefs of the world are as valuable as the truths of Christianity. His lies—mounted in settings of those things considered precious by the standards of the world—can keep us from seeing that which is of eternal worth. It would be the mistake of a lifetime to buy into such a fake bill of goods. We must keep a clear perspective of what is truly valuable.

The story of Jacob and Esau in the Bible demonstrates how people lose forever their greatest blessings because they never learned to appreciate their value. The story of these feuding twins has become a warning signal for every person living in the modern world.

As you may remember, Esau, the older brother of Jacob, had his birthright and blessing deceitfully taken from him by his younger brother. How could he have been so foolish as to not protect that which meant so much in his life and in the lives of the Israelites to come?

Unfortunately, a lot of people are permanently remembered for something—maybe just one thing—they did *wrong*. Bill Buckner played twenty-two years in the major league and had an impressive lifetime batting average of .289. What most sports enthusiasts remember about Buckner, however, is the sixth game of the 1986 World Series between Buckner's Boston Red Sox and the New York Mets. The score was tied at the bottom of the tenth inning, with two outs and a runner on third. Mookie Wilson hit an easy, routine ground ball that went right between the legs of the first baseman, Buckner, enabling Ray Knight to score from third base. The Mets won Game Six to tie the series and Game Seven to become world champions.

Bill Buckner is not alone in being remembered for a big mistake. Richard Nixon's presidency is remembered for Watergate. Fallen televangelists are remembered for their indiscretions. Some people's lives are forever marked by their one outstanding mistake or instance of poor judgment.

This is true of the men and women of the Bible, as well. None is more notable for his mistake than Esau. The writer of Hebrews sets him apart as an example: "See that no one is . . . godless like Esau, who for a single meal sold his inheritance rights as the oldest son" (Heb. 12:16).

Esau will always be remembered for his near-sightedness and his one big mistake. His misplaced sense of what mattered forever stands as a reminder to us who are so prone to stumble in the same way.

DYSFUNCTIONAL SAINTS

In some ways I think that Esau gets a bad rap. Most people think of Jacob as the good and godly wonder boy, and Esau as the devil himself. I don't want to minimize Esau's mistake, but as far as we can tell from the biblical account, Esau earned his place in the "immoral and godless" category primarily because of his foolishness and short-sightedness. By today's standards, he does not seem like such a bad guy. He was an outdoorsman, a hunter, and an athlete. If he lived in our generation, he would probably be characterized as "a real man's man."

An easy and commonly made paternal mistake is to favor one son over the other. Many times this happens when men want to live out their sports fantasies through their sons. They focus all their attention on the son who is a great athlete, making the other children feel second-rate. It was, perhaps, Isaac's selective approval that gave Esau his misplaced sense of values.

Jacob, whom we associate as being one of the good guys, was from the beginning anything but that. His very name meant "supplanter," or, in modern terms, "someone who will stab you in the back when you're not looking." Jacob could be described as a momma's boy who had an appreciation of and a proclivity toward domestic life. It is obvious he was intelligent and cunning. It is equally obvious he was envious of his brother's birthright.

Larry Crabb, in his book *Inside Out*,[4] points out that mothers often step in to shelter the child who is rejected by the father. This may have been the case with Jacob's mother, Rebekah. Isaac, Rebekah, Esau, Jacob, and their descendants turned out to be one of the most significant families in history. Yet they were anything but perfect. In fact, they were the classic dysfunctional family. Isaac's misplaced values inherited by Esau and Rebekah's deceitfulness passed on to Jacob caused their home to disintegrate.

IRRETRIEVABLE LOSSES

Jacob's envy and resentment of his older twin brother festered for years. The opportunity "to get one up" on him presented itself one afternoon when Esau, famished, came in from the fields. Jacob had a pot of stew cooking and saw the chance to strike a bargain with his hungry brother.

"Please, let me have a taste of some of that red stuff," requested Esau.

Jacob, ready to seize the opportunity, said, "First, sell me your birthright."

"Well, as you can see, I am about to die," said Esau. "What good is the birthright to me?"

"First, swear to me," Jacob persisted.

"So he swore an oath to him, selling his birthright to Jacob. Then Jacob gave Esau some bread and some lentil stew. He ate and drank, and then got up and left. So Esau despised his birthright" (Gen. 25:33–34).

To say that Esau "despised his birthright" doesn't necessarily mean he didn't want to have it. It simply indicates that he did not understand or appreciate the value of it. He was so near-sighted (or short-sighted) that he valued something to satisfy his immediate appetite more than his most precious possession, his birthright.

As citizens of a twentieth-century constitutional republic, it is hard for us to appreciate the significance of the birthright. It meant that the oldest son was destined to receive a double portion of the inheritance and would eventually be the patriarch of the clan. He would possess great authority and honor. The laws that have, for thousands of years, governed the right of succession of monarchies have their origins in the ancient family birthright.

The closest analogy in our modern times to Esau and his family is the British monarchy. Charles, the Prince of Wales, is first in line for succession to the throne after his mother, Queen Elizabeth. What Esau did would be comparable to Prince Charles coming in from losing a polo match, distracted by his problems with Di, and starving to death. He would be so hungry and upset that he foolishly trades his right to be king, and its accompanying riches and power, to his little brother, Andrew, for a big, juicy hamburger and a side of chips. It would be ludicrous!

There were two major mistakes for which Esau will always be remembered. First, he sold his birthright and, second, he lost the family blessing. Isaac knew the day of his death was fast approaching, and he sent his beloved son, Esau, out to kill some game and prepare a meal for him. At this meal, Isaac intended to give his blessing to Esau. You know the story—Jacob and his mother prepared a meal for Isaac, and Jacob disguised himself as his brother. In doing so, Jacob stole Esau's blessing.

It wasn't long before Esau realized what Jacob had done. "When Esau heard his father's words, he burst out with a loud and bitter cry and said to his father, 'Bless me—me too, my father! . . . Isn't he rightly named Jacob? He has deceived me these two times: He took my birthright, and now he's taken my blessing!'" (Gen. 27:34, 36).

The blessing was given to Jacob, and there was nothing left for Esau. "Esau said to his father, 'Do you have only one blessing, my father? Bless me too, my father!' Then Esau wept aloud" (Gen. 27:38).

Esau was a "good ole boy" who will tragically be remembered for his big mistake. He has become God's eternal example of a person who loses the blessings of life because of a short-sighted perspective. Either he never realized what really mattered in his life, or if he did understand, he lost sight of it in the light of his immediate desires.

The writer of Hebrews comments on the finality of Esau's tragedy: "Afterwards, as you know, when he wanted to inherit this blessing, he was rejected. He could bring about *no change of mind*, though he sought the blessing with tears" (12:17, italics mine).

Isaac could not change his mind and give the blessing to Esau, even though Esau cried out and wept bitterly for it. Esau is like many today who foolishly give away their birthrights and have the blessings of their lives stolen right out from under them. Their misplaced sense of value and perspective causes them to lose their families, their health, their integrity, and their usefulness in this world. Only when it's gone do they realize what they have lost, but by then it's too late. No matter how hard they try, they can't get it back.

HEAVEN'S GATE

How did Jacob change from a deceiver to the patriarch of the twelve tribes of Israel? How was his perspective of God and life's priorities so radically changed? It seems it would have taken "a truckload of bricks falling from the sky" to have gotten his attention—or maybe, just the gateway of heaven opening up and angels descending upon him!

Portals, or gateways, which can transport someone to another world or to another dimension of reality, are common literary themes—from ancient mythology to modern fiction. For example, the word *Babylon* literally means "the gate of the gods." Jesus referred to "the gates of hell." In C. S. Lewis's famous Christian allegory, *The Lion, the Witch and the Wardrobe*, the children discovered that they could go through the back of the old wardrobe and travel into another dimension of time and space, to the land of Narnia. That was their "portal" to Narnia.

The first mention of a portal or gate to heaven in Scripture was in the story of Jacob's dream at Bethel. Sometimes when we read or hear sermons about Jacob, his deceptions and trickery are excused because of his "godly desire" for the birthright and the blessing—which may be over-spiritualizing the situation. Jacob was no paradigm of righteousness. His deceitfulness seems to have been driven by jealousy, revenge, and a lust for power and money. Part of his motivation he got on his own, and part was planted in him by his mother.

Esau was so enraged by what his brother had done, he threatened to kill Jacob. Jacob was forced to flee for his life. As he was fleeing from Esau, on his way to Haran, Jacob camped at a place

11

called Luz. It was there God gave him the dream of a ladder set on the earth with its top reaching to heaven and with angels ascending and descending on it (see Gen. 28:12). We have come to refer to it as "Jacob's Ladder." Jacob awoke from his dreams and said: "'Surely the LORD is in this place, and I was not aware of it. . . . How awesome is this place! This is none other than the house of God; this is the *gate of heaven'*" (Gen. 28:16–17, italics mine).

There is nothing in the biblical account of Jacob's early life which suggests he was an exceptionally godly person. Perhaps he worshiped the God of his father and grandfather, Isaac and Abraham, but it may have been only out of rote or because of family tradition. What he had only heard about and tentatively believed, now became real and personal to Jacob. He named the place Bethel, which means "house of God." There he dedicated his life to God. The priorities and perspective of Jacob's life were changed as a result of coming upon a true heavenly portal.

No matter how optimistic, appreciative, or blessed individuals might be, it is only through an encounter with God that true peace and happiness come. If they don't personally know the love and saving grace of Jesus Christ, they have every reason to despair— for what they consider a true perspective of life is only a false illusion. This is the irony and deceitfulness of this present age. Those who should be utterly despairing over the purposelessness and futility of their lives are often falsely comforted by the gods of this age.

MATCH POINT

There were four defining moments in the life of Jacob:

1. buying his brother's birthright

2. stealing his brother's blessing

3. seeing heaven's gate

4. wrestling with God

The first three I have already discussed. The fourth was the mold-breaker and, ultimately, the man-maker.

Years later, Jacob came to the realization he had to face his past and be reconciled with his brother. He was on the journey home, with all his family, servants, and possessions, when night fell and he instructed the entourage to pitch camp across the stream. He remained on the opposite side of the stream, alone. It was the night before he was to meet his brother Esau. Shortly after falling asleep, he had an encounter with the angel of the Lord. Jacob wrestled with the angel until morning. The angel did not prevail in this bout and, consequently, touched Jacob's thigh, dislocating his hip joint. Still Jacob refused to let the angel go saying, "'I will not let you go unless you bless me'" (Gen. 32:26). He finally came to the realization that the true source of blessing in life is God! "The man asked him, 'What is your name?' 'Jacob,' he answered. Then the man said, 'Your name will no longer be Jacob, but Israel, because you have struggled with God and with men and have overcome'" (Gen. 32:27–28).

Jacob provides an excellent example of a person's coming to an understanding of what matters most in life. It is often necessary to wrestle with God and with the circumstances of life to receive the desired blessing. The process is life changing.

Jacob's name was changed because he had an experience with God and was transformed into a man of God. He walked with a limp for the rest of his life because he had been touched by God. In other words, he was never able to forget the match point.

KEEPING LIFE IN PERSPECTIVE

I recently walked through a shopping mall and noticed a phenomenon I have seen on several occasions. People were gathered around a cart, staring at framed prints. These people were squinting and turning their heads sideways. They had that I-just-don't-get-it look on their faces. They were trying to focus on three-dimensional images hidden in the dot configurations of simple repeating, computer-generated patterns, called "autosterograms."

At first glance, one of these pictures looks like a wallpaper pattern, but hidden in it is a picture within the picture. The trick is to be able to gain the proper perspective to see what others miss. Some people use the technique of placing the picture right on their nose and then slowly moving it away from their eyes. The key, others say, is to focus your eyes beyond the picture in your hand. It's not easy to do because your eyes do not naturally focus beyond the page.

When a person suddenly sees the image you'll hear them exclaim, "Oh, wow! There it is!" Then to all the others who have not seen it, they will boast, "It's easy, just relax your eyes and focus beyond the page." Yet even after you've seen the image, it is hard to keep it in focus. Suddenly it'll just go away, and all you can see is the repeating pattern.

Every time I see someone looking at one of those pictures it reminds me how hard it is to keep our lives in perspective. It's hard to focus beyond the ever-pressing realities of our daily lives. Even after we get our eyes focused so we can see the real picture, it is hard to maintain that viewpoint. We lose the true spiritual picture and again only see the meaningless repetition of the patterns of life.

Our struggles with the challenges of life are often wrestling matches with our own perspective. If we could see things the way God sees them, we would gain victory over all the elements that depress us, defeat us, and rob from us God's blessing. Like Elisha, whose eyes were opened to see the chariots of fire, we, too, need to have our eyes opened to the heavenly perspective. It is essential in our appreciating and attaining what truly matters in life and in our maintaining a proper and godly perspective of life.

PART ONE

DISTORTING OUR PERSPECTIVE

CHAPTER TWO

OUR PERSPECTIVE OF CHANGE

Many people reminisce about the "good ol' days." Whenever you hear that kind of talk, keep in mind they were never as good as people remember them to be! I look back on my childhood with fond memories; yet, those good ol' days were probably not as good as the picture I have of them in my mind. My family definitely did not enjoy the conveniences my children or grandchildren enjoy. I am not just talking about fancy electronic gadgets, but basic conveniences.

THE GOOD OL' DAYS?

During my early adolescent years, my family had only one bathroom—and we shared it with another family! We lived in a duplex which housed two families. Our family had two children—my brother Joe and me. The other family had one child—a girl, Teresa, who was about my age. As important as it was for us guys to have our privacy, it was even more important for Teresa. Yet that didn't stop me from banging on the bathroom door and making all sorts of inquiries of her—some urgent, some not too appropriate. It was great when we finally moved from there into a house with no shared facilities.

I don't often think about these things. I usually remember the good times and forget some of the inconveniences and challenges of the past. However, it might be beneficial to remember the past as it truly was.

Talk with people who have memories of the Depression, and you will discover, without a doubt, things are much better today. For example, the middle-class people in those days experienced a life which was much more difficult and less pampered than our present-day middle-class. If they were fortunate enough to have central heating (less than one-third did), someone—usually the dad—had to get out of bed at four o'clock on cold winter mornings to shovel coal. If he overslept, the pipes might freeze and burst. Also, for more than half the population in America, the family toilet was a hole in the back yard with a shack over it. Yes, times have really changed!

Back in 1921, the average workweek for typical Americans was sixty hours, and many worked longer. Recreation and entertainment industries didn't exist because most people didn't have any leisure time. Today, most poor families in America have many more creature comforts than middle-class citizens had fifty years ago.[1]

Memories can be deceiving. We color the way we remember bygone days. It is similar to the way I remember my basketball days. I wasn't quite tall enough to be considered the big man on our basketball team. You see, I'm just under 6'7"—about a foot under. I was, however, an important part of the team. I was the twelfth man on a twelve-man roster and what might be called "the encourager position." My job, played from the bench position, was to cheer on my teammates and keep them encouraged. The other players would look at my game, compare it to theirs, and feel encouraged! I did my job well. To tell the honest to goodness truth, I got discouraged because of too much time on the bench and not enough time on the court, so I put away my high tops and quit. I now wish I hadn't because the older I get the better player I remember I used to be. Give me another ten years or so and I'll be telling you about my twelve dunks in the championship game!

No doubt things are vastly different today than the way I remember them fifty years ago. In many ways we have it better than ever. Nowadays, kids start to moan and groan when they hear Grandpa retelling stories of walking five miles to school, one-way, barefooted, in a snowstorm! I recall my dad telling me about walking or riding a horse to school each day. His stories usually came about the time I'd bemoan the fact that I had to walk to school, sometimes in the bitter cold. (In fact, my family did not have a car until my junior year of high school. I did not get my first car until I was out of college.)

Dad told about one time he walked some distance to see his girlfriend. I guess he must have been distracted by his courting and failed to notice the snowstorm coming his way. Well, the snowstorm hit. He was stranded. Some time passed and my grandparents got concerned. To his embarrassment, this grown young man had to be rescued by his father—on horseback. Somehow, today's teens can't relate. (My son had his own pick-up truck by the time he was seventeen years old.)

If it's true then that we are living at the pinnacle of history, why are so many people sad, discontent, and depressed? I believe part of the answer lies in how we have responded to the tremendous changes which have occurred, especially over the last fifty to seventy-five years. Our modern society has experienced change in three major ways. They can be called the signs of our time.

SIGNS OF OUR TIME

SIGN 1: COMING IN FROM THE COUNTRY

One of the biggest changes in American life has been the move of people from the country into towns and cities. I vividly remember some of the best times of my life when I, as a boy, visited my grandparents who lived on farms outside of Nashville. There was nothing like sleeping in the loft and hearing the rain on the tin roof. I loved walking about their farms as I picked peaches, pears, cherries, apples, and strawberries for personal consumption, followed by drinks of cold well-water from a gourd. I'll never forget the smell of meat curing in the smokehouse, corn cob fights, walking in the woods and chasing squirrels, and the peaceful silence.

I don't think there's anything inherently better about living in the country—or in the city. They both have their advantages. I do find one disadvantage, however, in city life. One of the effects of "coming in from the country" has been the isolation of most of us from many basic realities of life.

When questioned about what came to mind when they heard the expression, "He's running around like a chicken with his head cut off," a group of teenagers said they thought of a frantic human—not a chicken. When asked if they had ever seen a chicken after its head had been chopped off, all said no, and most with a response like, "Oh, gross! No!"

We have created for ourselves a sanitized world. Although as a nation we certainly consume large quantities of chicken, most Americans have never rung one's neck or watched it running around the yard without its head. Of the 90 billion hamburgers McDonald's has supposedly sold, probably less than one out of a thousand were purchased by American customers who had ever seen a cow slaughtered.

Now I'm not suggesting we would all find the ideal existence by moving to the country. It's not that simple. It would drive some people crazy. It's too quiet in the day, and the katydids make too much noise at night. Plus, there are many benefits to living in the city. I am suggesting, nevertheless, that our move to the city has isolated people from many of the harsh and humbling realities of life which remind us of our common frailty and our dependence on God.

House needs cleaning? Car needs washing? Clothes need ironing? Yard needs mowing? House needs painting? Meals need preparing? We no longer have to deal with the unpleasantries of life; we can hire it done. We can get our needs met efficiently, allowing us free time to "enjoy life." We are made to feel like privileged kings (or queens).

Saul and David were the first two kings of Israel. Royalty was suddenly thrust upon them, much like the advantages which have so quickly come to Americans. Upon ascending the throne, Saul and David both faced the dilemma of handling a life of privilege without losing the perspective of their former life.

Just as the American people have moved in from the country, both Saul and David made the transition from their agrarian lifestyle to a regal lifestyle in the royal cities. They both went from living in modest country surroundings to living in the courts of a royal palace, at the very hub of political, social, and economic activity.

One of the most significant temptations kings face is the fact that they can basically do whatever they please. They are accountable to no higher authority. They can live a life of service or a life after the flesh. They can lead others to great achievements or be led to destruction by their own selfishness. Their use of newly acquired power can build or destroy what matters in their reign.

Several years ago one of the young men in our denomination was called to be pastor of one of the largest churches in the country. He had been serving as the pastor of a much smaller church and had little name recognition; yet suddenly, he was the talk on everybody's lips. Overnight, this fine young man became a celebrity.

Shortly thereafter, a few of my friends were in the presence of Dr. R. G. Lee, a wise leader and renowned preacher. The subject of this young preacher's elevation to his new pulpit came up. Dr. Lee's comment was simply, "Too much, too soon." He did not elaborate.

Dr. Lee's insight later proved true. It wasn't long before the pressures and temptations of power had forced the young pastor to resign under a cloud of suspicion and heartache.

Saul and David were not born with silver spoons in their mouths. They could remember simpler times, times when they were less independent and more dependent on others—especially God. *Dependence on God may be a hard lesson to convey to today's youth who have never lived a simpler lifestyle, who are a generation of privilege and convenience.*

SIGN 2: A GENERATION OF CONVENIENCE

We live in the most advanced society of all time. Life has never been easier nor more convenient. With automobiles, microwaves, refrigerators, dishwashers, computers, cell phones, and fax machines, we get more done with less effort. Most of us have more leisure time than any prior generation. The simple chore of washing clothes was quite an undertaking for our grandparents. What used to be a day-long project now requires only about an hour or two.

I am reminded of a story about an elderly lady, Virginia, who was known for her baking—especially for her delicious apple pies with their delicate crusts. This story occurred about the time paper plates were being introduced to American households. Virginia was so excited about these new throw-away plates, she bought some as soon as her grocer stocked them.

It was the week of the quarterly church box supper. She thought about what she should prepare and knowing what folks wanted, Virginia baked one of her pies. As she removed the pie from its cooking dish, she carefully placed it on one of her new paper plates. She soon realized it did not offer enough support for the weight of the dessert, so she placed the paper plate on top of a china plate. She sliced the pie and took it to the box supper to be

21

auctioned off to the highest bidder. A gentleman gave a generous contribution to the church fund to purchase the pie. He promptly sat down and dove his fork into a slice. As he ate the pie he had an increasingly perplexed look on his face. He struggled to swallow each bite. The look on his face made the woman inquire if there was something wrong with her dessert.

"I'm sorry, Ma'am," he said, "but this pie doesn't taste like yours usually does. I think the crust must have set up too hard or something."

Virginia examined the rest of the pie to see what the problem could possibly be, only to discover, to her horror, that when she had sliced the pie, she had also sliced the paper plate! The man had eaten a slice of the new paper plate along with his pie! I guess he had bitten off a little more than he could chew of that modern convenience!

Convenience is not always advantageous. Although we should thank God for conveniences because they enable us to set aside time to cultivate our inner life and to enjoy being with Him, there may be a downside. If the time restored to us for our relaxation, contemplation, and restoration is misused, the benefit is lost. Read the warning given to the church by the writer of the epistle of Hebrews: "We want each of you to show the same diligence to the very end, in order to make your hope sure. We do not want you to become lazy, but to imitate those who through faith and patience inherit what has been promised" (6:11–12).

This was written as a warning to believers to keep them from falling away from the faith. How very appropriate this message is for society—especially professing believers—today. I too often hear comments such as, "I can worship God just as well out on my boat. I don't need to be in a church on Sundays to be near God." Another modification goes something like, "I work so hard all week. I have no time to relax or to stay physically fit. I've always been taught that my body was the temple of the Holy Spirit. I owe it to God to use my Sundays to walk the golf course so that I can keep His temple in shape!"

Most of the free time created by our modern conveniences is filled up with entertainment. It has been said the average child spends seven hours a day watching television. We have become a society addicted to entertainment. We cannot be alone with ourselves for very long without needing something to entertain us. There are handheld video games and watch-sized television sets so a person waiting somewhere to be served or transported will not have to wait silently and unoccupied.

Americans spent $340 billion in 1993 on entertainment. From 1991 to 1993, consumers increased their spending on recreation and entertainment by 13 percent, more than twice the rate of increase in overall spending.[2] This spending pattern continues to escalate in response to demand. The effect of entertainment consumption on society is a numbing distraction from the important things in life.

Saul allowed his kingly power and privilege to become a drain on his inner life. He sought entertainment to numb the pain and heal the stress of being king. In fact, for a time, David was one of his court musicians. When Saul experienced severe depression, he called out for David, rather than crying out to God. "Whenever the spirit from God came upon Saul, David would take his harp and play. Then relief would come to Saul; he would feel better, and the evil spirit would leave him" (1 Sam. 16:23).

Just the opposite was true of David. When he was depressed or discouraged, he himself would compose a psalm of his discontent and sing it over and over to the Lord. David needed no outsider to help him express his innermost feelings to God. In these psalms, he alternately poured out his distress and then expressed his confidence in the sovereign God. "Be merciful to me, O LORD, for I am in distress; my eyes grow weak with sorrow, my soul and my body with grief. My life is consumed by anguish and my years by groaning; . . . But I trust in you, O LORD; I say, 'You are my God.' My times are in your hands" (Ps. 31:9–10, 14–15).

There came a point in Saul's life as king when his inner life was so depleted he no longer had the strength to write or sing his own song. He could only listen to David's. David's music was like a spiritual dialysis machine which would do for Saul's soul what his own inner man could no longer do.

Saul eventually was consumed by jealousy for David. David was forced to run and hide from him. When David felt abandoned by others and by God, and he could find no answer or direction, again he cried out to the Lord through psalms. At the time he was hiding from Saul in a cave, he wrote what is now called the Fifty-seventh Psalm. "Have mercy on me, O God, have mercy on me, for in you my soul takes refuge. I will take refuge in the shadow of your wings until the disaster has passed. I cry out to God Most High, to God, who fulfills his purpose for me" (Ps. 57:1–2).

When Saul felt the same way, he had no such ability, desire, or patience. After he forced David to flee, Saul cried out to Samuel the prophet; when God removed Samuel, Saul sought out the witch of Endor (see 1 Sam. 28). He no longer knew how to seek God on his own.

The conveniences we enjoy today can, likewise, alienate us from God. As a generation of privilege, we must take great care in how we use our time. Do we fill the hours with numbing entertainment, or do we productively establish a discipline of knowing and serving God, to whom we can turn in our time of need. How we use our time speaks volumes about our determination to have a personal relationship with Him. It is much like a checkbook; when our leisure time is examined, it reveals just how much has actually been spent for godly pursuits. We each should examine our days. *Are modern conveniences, especially entertainment, keeping us from God, from the right perspective on life?*

SIGN 3: THE WORLD AT OUR DOORSTEP

Wherever my travels take me, there's always CNN to connect me with home and the rest of the world. In the morning when I open the door of an out-of-town hotel room, at my door is a copy of *USA Today,* so I can stay in touch. Whether I am on a plane or on a ship, in the States or abroad, there's always a telephone so I can reach out and touch someone. The world has gotten much smaller.

As it shrinks, our mobility increases. If we're fortunate enough to be able to board the Concord and jet from New York to London, we can do so in three hours. If we're in a distant city and need a signature on a document today, it can be accomplished via fax machine. If we need to reach someone who is not at home or at the office, there are always call-forwarding, voice mail, beepers, and cellular phones. Let's not forget accessibility through e-mail and the worldwide Internet. The world is at our doorsteps.

The world at our doorsteps, however, is overwhelming in many aspects. Times have changed from the days of getting the news from the town barber during a hair cut or from crossed telephone party lines. Weekly newspapers featured a much smaller community with less diversity and considerably less controversy. It was simple. Folks cared about their neighbors and their community. If someone was in need, they stopped what they were doing and pitched in to help out.

Now, with the world brought into our homes, it is getting awfully crowded. How do we begin to know whom to help or what help is possible for us to give? How much is enough? Where do we even begin?

Every generation in every century before this one has had its own burdens to bear, and, in reality, these burdens may have been much greater than ours. Their burdens, however, were for their neighbors, their friends, and their communities. Now the media tells us that for us to be politically correct we must rally to the cause of every special interest group and every endangered species worldwide. We are told that the earth is ours and we must care for the ozone layer, the diminishing rain forests, AIDS victims, war refugees, drug problems of our youth, rising taxes, the elderly, and the decline of family life in America! Violence is on the rise, and the news constantly reminds us that our fellow man is out to get us.

Somehow, I think this constant diet of national, and even international, tragedies and events has caused people to turn inward and build walls around themselves and their families. Adopting a survivalist mentality, we deadbolt the lock on the doors of our lives, load the shotgun to protect ourselves against the desperate acts of others, and dare anyone to come on our property. None of us can carry the burdens of the entire world, but, sadly, fewer and fewer of us understand what it really means to "love thy neighbor." We have shut out others.

Recently, I noticed a For Sale sign in the yard of a man who lived two doors down from me. A few days after the sign went up, I saw him walking his dog and asked about the sign. He said he and his wife were moving to another state to be close to family and friends for the latter days of their lives. We said our good-byes, and I walked away feeling rather grieved. Here was an older man and his wife who live a few hundred feet from me. I had scarcely ever done more than say hello and exchange a little small talk. Now they were moving halfway across the country to be around family, friends and neighborly people. I felt I had personally failed him and his wife. After all, the Bible says, "Love your neighbor as yourself" (Lev. 19:18), and this couple were certainly my neighbors—in the most literal sense.

Saul and David both lost the perspective of what was best for their families, their neighbors, and themselves after becoming preoccupied with selfish desires and less attuned to God's guidance.

25

They were so preoccupied with national and international attention they neglected the needs of those closest to them.

For Saul, it was his egocentric desire to regain national popularity which forced him to be consumed with jealousy for David. Hearing the people's chant, "Saul has slain his thousands, and David his tens of thousands," drove Saul to neglect what was best for Israel, his son Jonathan, and his personal relationship with God in his quest to destroy David (see 1 Sam. 18:6–9).

For David, after numerous successful military campaigns, he was content to stay back at the palace, no longer serving God in the ways previously blessed by God, letting others come and serve him. He indulged his selfish desires of having anything in the world he wanted to the point of attaining the possession he could not rightfully have—the wife of another man. His abuse of power in securing Bathsheba's presence at his Jerusalem residence, in commanding sexual favors from her, and then in orchestrating her husband's death in battle was an inherent danger of being king.

Becoming a king of the generation of privilege tends to alter our perspective of the important matters in life. Unfortunately, most kings, with time, conclude *they* are what really matters in their kingdom. In the same way, when we allow ourselves to be overly served and excessively honored, it affects the way we view ourselves. Most of us, if the truth were known, are not capable of handling fame or success.

How do we maintain the delicate balance between serving God and serving self, caring for the world and being overwhelmed by all the cares of the world? Our perspective has everything to do with this. We must keep our eyes firmly fixed on God, not on self, and allow Him to open our eyes to the needs of others. We must trust Him to expand our service to others as it serves *Him* best. If we try to do all and be all, we may end up depressed and discouraged, like Saul and David.

Our church has an annual time of foreign missions emphasis. As a part of this emphasis, flags from all over the world are flown in our worship center. We fly black flags to represent countries where the message of Jesus Christ is not allowed. Because, as a congregation, we take seriously the Great Commission mandate (see Matt. 28:19–20), we want desperately to reach a lost and dying world for our Lord. This accepted responsibility to reach so many nations for the Lord can be overwhelming, to say the least.

Where do we begin? How can we possibly do it all? Do we give up because we can't possibly do it all? As pastor, my desire is to be sensitive to the leadership of the Holy Spirit in helping God's people select missions goals for our church. One way we have helped our folks get a handle on missions is by posting a sign at the main exit of our church. It reads, "You are now entering the mission field." The idea behind this sign is to encourage people to take a first step and to start at home with their mission efforts. The world is awfully large to hold in our hands. We must leave this job to God.

Riddle: *Do you know how you eat an elephant?* Answer: *One bite at a time!* So it must be in caring for our world. Love our neighbor—more than self.

INNER CHANGE

The three signs of our times which we just considered are not inherently evil. There is nothing wrong with living in the city with all the modern conveniences or being connected to the world via CNN and the Internet. These can be of great service to us, but they can also be a drain on our inner lives.

In 1983, I took my first sabbatical. The previous twelve months had been exhausting. One daughter had gotten married, and the other had graduated from college. I had participated in a Billy Graham crusade. To top it off, we had relocated our church from the downtown area to our present location. I had a desperate need for a break. The church graciously gave me a few weeks off, and a generous couple offered the use of their cabin in the mountains of North Carolina.

The cabin was rustic looking but comfortable. There was no paved road, only a pathway barely wide enough for a car. The cabin was at the far end of that path. The first week I nearly went crazy trying to rest. It was too quiet and too still.

Finally, I did settle down. I spent much time walking, thinking, and reflecting, even about my own restlessness. One day I sat on the porch watching a colony of ants dissect a dead wasp. I was enthralled and fascinated by the wonder of God's creation. It eventually dawned on me how much time I had spent simply watching those ants. Only God knows how much we miss because we never sit still and just be with ourselves and with God.

Even as I write this chapter, I am reminded of this very thing. For the last few days, I have enjoyed helping lead a Bible study cruise, an annual event. As I sought a quiet spot on the deck to work on this manuscript, I overheard several passengers discussing their desire to find the ideal vantage point from which to watch our ship's departure from the beautiful Bahamian port. Now, as I sit here, I realize *I* am probably sitting at that perfect spot from which to enjoy God's spectacular tropical landscape. I must confess, however, I almost missed it because I had my head down in my notes. I was concentrating so intently on what He would have me say that I almost forgot to look up and look out at what He would have me see. Do you ever have that same problem of missing God's simple—yet profound—pleasures in life because you, too, are so busy with doing *His work?*

Many of us would be terrified if we thought we had to go back and live in the world of the nineteenth century. No television, no cell phones, no video games, and no NBA "Game of the Week." If we wanted chicken for dinner, we would have to kill it. If we wanted to get a message to someone, we would have to write a letter. If we wanted to enjoy music, we would have to play an instrument. If we had any leisure time in which to be entertained, we could not go to the movies; we would have to read a book.

As time has passed, modernity, while affording us many creature comforts and expanded horizons, contributed to our gradual dying on the inside—like Saul. The symptoms have been masked as we have been hooked up to so many new-fangled life-support systems. On numerous occasions, I, as a pastor, have had to visit hospital intensive care units. I have witnessed time and again patients with tubes coming out of the bodies and with wires attached to machinery—all for the purpose of life support for these individuals. Their bodies could no longer sustain life without external help. We, too, have found artificial living through our external attachments to all that time has afforded us. We are often oblivious to our deteriorating condition on the inside.

We can be entertained but cannot entertain ourselves. We can watch sporting events, but we cannot play. We can proclaim, "Go for the gusto," but, while on the go, we have lost the ability to live with ourselves—hence, the lack of true satisfaction that often accompanies the accumulation of things and the access to privilege.

A missionary was telling about a birthday party in a new Ukrainian church. There were no professional clowns, musicians, or magicians. Instead, each person there, from the oldest to the youngest, took turns singing, dancing, and acting out dramas. The American team members were amazed. Entertainment was something these people *did,* not hired. They were inner-life producers rather than inner-life consumers.

The lives of the two kings, Saul and David, were parallel in many respects. They were both chosen by God and anointed by the prophet Samuel to sit on Israel's throne. There was no indication of any spiritual deficiency in either of them; in fact, the opposite appears true. Before he became king, Saul was used by God and numbered with the prophets (see 1 Sam. 10:9–11). We are even more familiar with David's being used by God to defeat a mighty foe, Goliath (see 1 Sam. 17:45–50).

There was a point of departure, however, from their common path. It became evident, in a matter of time, that the lives of these two kings were headed in drastically different directions. Saul's life took a different course when he began to seek his will over and above God's will. He allowed the power and privilege available to him to drain his inner life. In the end, he was almost completely dead on the inside. David, on the other hand, kept a pretty steady course. Yes, he made some serious mistakes, as did Saul, and took at least one major detour from the path God had chosen for him. Yet, he regained his footing and maintained his direction in following God's course for him as king. His inner life continued to grow in the midst of the pressures similar to ours today.

Most of us prefer to identify with David, the man after God's heart, rather than desperate Saul. As Gene Edwards points out in his marvelous little book *The Tale of Three Kings,*[3] there is a little of both of these kings in us all. It is critical, therefore, for us, as believers, to constantly seek God's strength for our lives and to continually be renewed through His abiding presence in us.

Through the early years of my life and ministry, my devotional life was like a roller coaster with its ups and downs in consistency. I'd try morning devotions, evening devotions, noon-time devotions—anything to carve out a slot to replenish my inner being in my busy schedule. My time with God, nevertheless, was always inconsistent or even neglected. I began to come in contact with people who had deeper walks with God for which I longed. I loved talking to these people, but I was painfully convicted of my own shallowness and superficiality when I compared my walk with God to theirs.

It all came to a climax when I was threatened with a lawsuit because of a public stand I had taken on a moral issue in our community. I was troubled and full of anxiety, manifesting little of the peace I had seen in others. One of those people whose walk with God I so admired came into my office one day.

29

"I don't know what it is," he said, "but I just felt I was supposed to come and pray for you."

As he knelt to pray he put his hands on me. It felt like the warmth of a fireplace spreading from his hands across my shoulders into my body. It was like a quiet river washing over my mind and my heart. A new strength was birthed in me! That was one of the turning points in my commitment to Christ. I was determined that my devotional life would, from that point on, be first priority. I was committed to staying plugged into the true source of my strength and joy.

The temptation of the modern world is to access the innumerable opportunities to stimulate us by external means. We must find personal renewal and fulfillment by turning inward—not looking to self, but to the Holy Spirit to renew and refresh us.

I certainly don't see myself as any kind of king, but I have experienced, in small measure, something of what presidents, athletes, celebrities, and political leaders experience on a regular basis. I remember well the feeling I had when I received the call in my hotel room informing me I had been elected president of the Southern Baptist Convention (SBC). My life was about to change. My ministry was about to take a dramatically new direction. Jeanette and I immediately got on our knees and prayed. We submitted ourselves to God's lordship. We sought His guidance and wisdom as we sought to be His representatives in the leadership of the Convention.

The next thing I knew a sheriff's deputy was knocking at the door. We got up and were escorted immediately to a large press conference. Following that, everywhere we went, the deputy stayed with us—driving us and guarding us throughout the convention. That was a unique experience, certainly like nothing to which we were accustomed.

Because of the presidency, I have had similar experiences since then. I am certain things will change when my term has expired. I remember what Dr. Herschel Hobbs said to former SBC president, Jimmy Draper, as his term of office was expiring: "Do you see the road sign?" pointing to an exit sign. "That's what you will be after your term is over, an 'ex-It'!"

Both of these biblical kings had similar beginnings. Over time, living the life of a king caused something to die inside of Saul. David's royal lifestyle didn't have the same effect on him. David never forgot how to sing. Whether he was happy, sad, victorious, or defeated, he always poured his heart out to God. In his time with God, he discovered the source of abundant life.

The abundant life can be ours today. Change has brought us so many wonderful and useful conveniences that can, if properly viewed and managed, enhance our lives and our service to others. We must, however, examine our perspective of the privileges afforded us today and not allow them to rob us of the greatest treasure ever—a deep and abiding relationship with the Giver of all good and perfect gifts. We must be discerning in our use of His resources, lest we appreciate the gifts more than the Giver. Our inner beings can only be strengthened when we submit all facets of modern life to the true King of kings.

CHAPTER THREE

OUR PERSPECTIVE OF PRIORITIES

I remember, like it was yesterday, teaching my children to drive an automobile. When it came their turn to learn how to drive, I would take each of them to the cemetery or the church parking lot. There we would have a little one-on-one instruction. During one of those times, my oldest daughter, Kitty, was at the wheel. Nervous about this new undertaking, she mistakenly pushed the gas pedal instead of the brake. Consequently, she hit the corner of a stately, black wrought iron fence at the entrance to the church. That fence proved a better driving instructor than I! She never confused those pedals again.

A DRIVING TEST

I still laugh when I think of the driver's test I took at age sixteen to get my license. As I pulled out of the parking lot with the highway patrolman seated next to me, I gave the car a little too much gas. We zoomed onto the road to the roar of squealing tires and the smell of burnt rubber! I knew for certain I had failed the test. He must have been scared to ride with me again because he passed me!

Here's a "driving test"[1] for you. It is a quick inventory of the way you operate. Put a check by each one of the following statements you think is true about yourself. I'll leave it to you and the Lord to grade your paper; so, be honest.

___ I am very uncomfortable when the details of future events or activities are not planned.

___ I establish unrealistic goals and expectations and set myself up to feel like a failure.

___ I like to keep my emotions to myself.

___ I often feel guilty about relaxing.

___ Prayer is more difficult for me than Bible reading or going to church.

___ I plan out the coming week while sitting in church on Sunday mornings.

___ People can depend on me to get a job done.

___ Being on time for appointments is a priority for me.

___ I like to make lists.

___ I worry too much about things that never happen.

___ I seem to be emotionally in control on the surface, but when things don't go right, I am quick to get irritable and angry.

___ I often compare my own house, car, and clothes to those of my peers.

___ I do not like my job.

___ I'm really looking forward to retirement.

___ I feel very bad about myself when I don't perform well.

___ I sometimes am too busy to make it to important events in my child's life.

___ I have a hard time saying no to urgent requests for help.

___ I seldom feel like I have done enough.

___ I have a hard time trusting God.

___ I often live from one urgent demand to the next.

If ten of the twenty statements above apply to you, consider yourself to be a driven person. If you checked fifteen or more of the above, you are probably living a lifestyle that causes you to miss out on many of the very best things in life, the things that really matter. So, what drives you?

Dr. Robert Hemfelt tells a story about a man named Tony. The joy he should have felt from his numerous blessings was eaten away by Tony's addiction: he was a workaholic. Tony went into a treatment program for people with compulsive-addictive behavior patterns. In one stage of the program, the counselors had Tony view some of his family's home videos. As Tony watched, he saw, for the first time, his children's birthday parties, their first attempts at riding bicycles, their first dates, and so on. The tapes definitely had the intended effect on Tony. He couldn't believe he had missed all those things. Somewhere along the way Tony had misplaced his priorities.[2]

Often success is hollow. Bill McCartney was the football coach for the University of Colorado, a team that he saw crowned national champions. Everything seemed to be going great for McCartney. Therefore, people were surprised when McCartney, at the top of his profession, resigned and walked away from it all. One reason he shared for this career and life move was his desire to reprioritize his life. He said he felt he needed to get his life in order and his former commitments were keeping him from doing so.

Abundant life for busy people is a combination of focusing on high and lofty goals while keeping sight of the wonderful things they already possess. It is striving for that feeling of accomplishment while, at the same time, enjoying the process of getting there. As with anything else, going to either extreme may result in getting off course. For example, many driven people get bogged down in a quagmire of goal-setting, progress evaluations, and discontentment over where they are versus where they want to be. As a result, many people are like Tony. Life's greatest opportunities and experiences continually pass them by without their attention or appreciation.

THE MICRO-MEASUREMENTS OF SUCCESS

I had to laugh as I stood at a gasoline pump the other day. When I looked at the pump's meter, a thought occurred to me, *What possible benefit can anyone get out of knowing to the one-thousandth of a gallon the amount of gasoline they've just pumped?* I continued to think about this after I got home. I figured out that one one-thousandth of a gallon is less than one-half of a teaspoon. That's pretty insignificant. Yet, there it was on the meter. Someone had decided it was important for me to know that I got exactly 14.937 gallons of fuel at that fill-up.

We have become measurement fanatics. In our technologically advanced society, we have become accustomed to having instantaneous and precise measurements. With the formerly needed expertise of a nurse, we can now check our own pulse, blood pressure, temperature, and weight at home in a matter of seconds. We desire control over the smallest elements of our lives.

As a society, we also define meaning, self-worth, and personal significance in terms of measurable achievement. We have a very well-developed measuring stick that shows how well we each are doing. Cars, clothes, position, titles, club memberships, etc., are all measurements of our accomplishments and, unfortunately, our perceived worth. Though most of us would not subscribe to this type of value system, we, nevertheless, are affected by it. Many of us respond to this kind of consistent grading by becoming performance-oriented, goal-driven people.

Perhaps you are married to (or are yourself) someone who is totally caught up in the corporate world. To survive in this competitive, "bottom-line" environment, the driven person looks at everything in life as a challenge to conquer, a hill to take, or a game to win. Driving to church can even become a race to beat the car in the next lane. Vacations become projects to be managed on a Critical Path planning chart, complete with mission statements, approved budgets, and quality assurance. For pathological goal-setters, life revolves around long-range goals. They will bulldoze anything that gets in their way to success.

For these driven people, the unpardonable sin is wasting time. Time is money. If their time is not being used productively, they fidget nervously; their blood pressure rises until something sets them off like a volcano. Hell hath no fury like an executive whose schedule has been interrupted! Does any of this sound vaguely familiar? Have I described anyone you know?

This drivenness filters down to our children. A teacher told me about a student who was the product of driven parents. The child was frequently absent because of "a nervous stomach." When taking a test, she bites her bottom lip, twists her hair, and, if approached, bursts into tears. When asked about the tears, the child blamed them on her fear of not pleasing her parents. Concerned, the teacher requested a parent conference. Only the mother showed up; she explained that the father had gotten involved with a project at work and couldn't get away.

The mother went on to describe the stress level in their home. Things were pretty tense, to say the least. The child "somehow had imposed on herself perfectionistic tendencies" and was spending excessive amounts of time on all assignments, large or small. She would come home after school and go straight to her room to study, where she would remain for hours, trying to complete all the work missed when absent. She had to drop out of all extracurricular activities to handle her school work. On test days, the child

35

would come unglued prior to coming to school fearing she might not perform well and make the desired grade. (Consequently, the student often did fail to do her best because of her high stress level and the fact that she missed key concepts due to frequent absences.)

The mom had just taken her daughter to a physician who had prescribed medication to help her daughter's condition. The problem was affecting the whole family. Things weren't running as smoothly as they should in their household with a family member in turmoil. This just had to be fixed.

This is not an isolated situation according to other teaching professionals. We overly driven adults are passing our neurotic tendencies on to our children. In doing so, we are guaranteeing that the next generation will be as controlled by goal-setting as we are. What a legacy to pass on to subsequent generations.

JOY IN THE PROCESS

How many times have you taken a trip with children and every five miles or so one of them sticks his or her little head over the front seat and asks, "How much longer 'til we get there?" Children can be so anxious to get where they're going that they miss all the fun of the trip—and so does everyone traveling with them!

Likewise, impatience over what we, as adults, want in life can ruin the joy of the whole experience of traveling down life's way. One key to happiness in life seems to be learning to have joy in the process, not just in reaching the goal. The CEO of a large corporation, who had worked his way up from an entry-level position to the top, once commented, "The key to my success was that I never had a job I didn't love."

Similarly, on a PBS special, Bill Moyers asked Bill Gates, the then twenty-nine-year-old founder and president of Microsoft, "You have more money than you'll ever need. What makes you get up and go to work every day?"

Gates simply replied, "I love it!"

The title of Marsha Sinetar's 1989 book, *Do What You Love, the Money Will Follow* (Dell), echoes the sentiments of a lot of the people who are bailing out of the corporate world because their expectations have not been met. The illusive dream they were chasing on the way up somehow escaped their grasp. They worked so hard yet settled for so little personal fulfillment. She writes of their making a change to do what they thought they would love.

Frequently I discuss with people their goals and their dreams. Some say they dream of owning their own business; yet, few truly enjoy the hard work necessary to make it happen. There are others who want to have a book on the best-sellers list; however, few have come to love the act of writing. The dream and enjoyment of the process too often don't mesh.

What then is the answer? As the process often takes time, individuals must learn to find joy in the process. For example, parents who dream of having perfect kids should learn to love parenting. Salespeople who want to excel should not be content only in meeting sales quotas, but rather learn to find joy in meeting people's needs.

Until his retirement, Jimmy was the overall number one salesman for his national insurance company for more than thirty years When questioned about his success in sales, he replied, "I always treated people like I wanted to be treated. I really believed in my product, and I thought I was doing my clients a favor by honestly helping them meet their insurance needs. It gave me great joy to be there in their time of need with a policy that did for them what I had promised." Jimmy loved the process.

This, however, is not always the case in people's lives. It is disturbing to see people who spend their entire lives hating what they do, but persevering just to obtain a retirement check. It is equally sad to see people who have come to the realization that their dreams will never come true. That is the nature of many people's mid-life crises. Sometimes the crisis comes from achieving everything for which they have striven only to find the expected pay-off is a modicum of success, superficial and short-lived.

Many draw up "honey-do" lists for their spouses. The problem with these lists is that they continue to grow as quickly as items are checked off! So it is with our lives; no matter how many goals we check off, somehow we never arrive. Would it really hurt to sometimes pause and say to ourselves, "This is it! I've arrived! It just doesn't get any better than this"? Understand, I know that things might get better, or, who knows, they might not. Wouldn't it be sad if the greatest times of our lives were spent wistfully dreaming about how good it will be when we finally get somewhere else?

I recall watching Bill Cosby in a made-for-TV movie about a man whose son had sickle-cell anemia. They had done everything they could for their son, but the doctor gave no hope for the boy.

The father was walking with his son by the beach trying to find words to explain the doctor's prognosis. The little boy looked up and said, "Daddy, are you trying to tell me that I'm going to die?"

"Yes," his father said. After a few moments of silence, he continued, "But, Son, there are three kinds of people in the world; yesterday's people, tomorrow's people, and today's people. From this point on, you, Mom, and I are going to be today's people."

We all need to savor life in the present, to enjoy the process and be a today's person. Yes, our goals are for the future, but we must strive to live in the moment.

FOUR SYMPTOMS OF THE MARTHA FACTOR

The kind of drivenness about which I am writing is, perhaps, more common today than at any other time in history. Nevertheless, it did not have its roots in the modern age. There have always been people whose self-worth depended on their performance, people who were success- or goal-driven to the point of failing to appreciate what was right at hand. Martha, the sister to Mary and Lazarus and the friend of Jesus, was one such person.

Mary and Martha were two very different personalities. Their approaches to life and living serve as mirrors, reflecting the way we deal with the demands and opportunities of everyday life. Martha was a person all twentieth-century people need to examine closely. She was the sister who focused on attaining goals and taking care of business to the point of missing out on the present. Mary, on the other hand, was an individual who perceived the value of things happening around her. Mary captured the moment before it slipped away and then lived it for all it was worth.

> As Jesus and his disciples were on their way, he came to a village where a woman named Martha opened her home to him. She had a sister called Mary, who sat at the Lord's feet listening to what he said. But Martha was distracted by all the preparations that had to be made. She came to him and asked, "Lord, don't you care that my sister has left me to do the work by myself? Tell her to help me!" "Martha, Martha," the Lord answered, "you are worried and upset about many things, but only one thing is needed. Mary has chosen what is better, and it will not be taken away from her." (Luke 10:38–42)

Martha probably was older than her sister, Mary, and her brother, Lazarus. Perhaps she was a widow, and it was for this reason her home was referred to as "Martha's house." They lived in

Bethany, a small village on the eastern slope of the Mount of Olivet, about two miles from Jerusalem. It was a place Jesus frequently visited.

Jesus was on His way to Jerusalem for the Feast of Dedication. By this point in His earthly ministry, it had grown dangerous to be associated with Him—much less entertain Him, especially so near Jerusalem. Undaunted, Martha opened her home to her dear friend, Jesus. She was somewhat annoyed that Mary was sitting at Jesus' feet listening to His words while she (Martha) was working so hard on the preparations.

Things certainly seemed to be out of order. First of all, if, in fact, Mary was the younger of the two, she should have been the one doing the work. In any case, it seems that she should have at least helped Martha.

Second, sitting at the feet of a rabbi or teacher was the traditional posture in a teacher-pupil relationship. For example, in another New Testament reference, Paul sat at the feet of Gamaliel (see Acts 22:3). In those days one would never expect a woman to take such a position—as if she was one of His immediate disciples.

During situations like this the true motivation of one's heart is often revealed, and such was the case with Martha. Jesus' words to Mary were not recorded. What seemed to be most important here was Jesus' response to Martha. His response revealed that her busy-ness and her disordered priorities, like those of many people today, were causing her to miss out on something of great importance. At least four symptoms of the Martha Factor stand out in this story. See if you can relate to any of these.

SYMPTOM 1: SHE WAS DISTRACTED BY HER PREPARATIONS

Jesus was coming to Martha's house with a dozen friends, probably without much, if any, advance notice. I'm sure most wives and mothers can identify with the pressure that was on Martha. We husbands, on the other hand, fail to understand what this does to a hostess's stress level.

I'm sure many pastors, like myself, have had similar experiences. I have called home at the last moment announcing to Jeanette that I'm bringing guests home for dinner. "You're doing WHAT?" is her frantic reply. "How can I clean the house and prepare a meal in thirty minutes?" It's important to her, like most wives, that everything be beautiful and in order. So, what does a good husband do in such a situation? I usually promise all sorts of things in exchange for this one huge favor and pledge "cross my heart and hope to die" to never do it again. Jeanette never lets me down. I'm always amazed when we get home. The house is spotless; the meal is terrific. You would think Jeanette had been planning all week for the visit. She stands there smiling a sweet smile as our guests walk in our home, followed by a piercing glance at me as I follow sheepishly behind them.

Most husbands don't understand why it's important to wives to have everything in the house so perfect. Listen up, husbands! Men who are driven by money and careers do the same thing as women who are driven to get the house ready for company. Both are striving to establish their worth and significance in what they do. Both are as likely to miss out on something important. Martha was so busy that she was not able to hear or concentrate on what Jesus was saying.

Likewise, today, busy-ness can distract Christians from pursuing growth in their relationship with Jesus Christ. Preoccupation with schedules, goals, and agendas can prevent believers from taking time to sit at the Master's feet. Prayer time is often shoved out of the way to make room for all the details of life.

I cannot recall all of the methods I have tried in getting others (and myself) to pray. I am not against prayer programs. I do know, however, that you can teach people to pray, exhort them to pray, and hold them accountable to pray, but, by and large, Christians still lack the discipline of prayer. For many, getting victory in this area may not come from a new method, but from the realization that the problem lies in their lifestyle. Twentieth-century Christians find themselves caught up in a pace of life that leaves no time for such things as prayer and meditation.

I remember going out to visit my grandparents when I was a boy. I have a picture in my memory, much like a Norman Rockwell painting, of both my grandfathers sitting in front of the general store, whittling. Much can be learned about the quality of a person's relationship with God by asking the question, "Can you whittle?" Let me explain what I mean. Whittling is quite different from carving, of course. When you are carving, the purpose is to fashion some object out of a piece of wood. Whittling is simply making a small stick out of a large stick. By asking the question, Can you whittle?, I am not referring to the skill required for whittling, but instead, I am asking, Can you bring yourself to sit down and whittle?

Somehow I can't picture Martha sitting down, whittling, and enjoying the words of her Friend. She was so consumed with all she had to do that she simply could not stop and concentrate on what Jesus was saying. Likewise, most of us today are distracted by our hectic lifestyles. To develop that consistent prayer life and to cultivate the ability to hear His voice, we must first deal with all the distractions and then learn how to be still. For Christians, prayer should be a privilege not a pressure. More than a discipline, it should be our heart's desire. For some, however, this is difficult. It is hard to sit still without a knee bouncing up and down or mental computers printing out things-to-do lists. We desperately need a time of solitude and stillness in which to come before God, without a pre-set agenda—simply a time to meditate, to pray, to think, to listen, or just to whittle.

Symptom 2: She Was Deceived About Her Duties

"'Martha, Martha,' the Lord answered, 'you are worried and upset about many things, but *only one thing is needed*. Mary has chosen what is better, and it will not be taken away from her'" (Luke 10:41 42, italics mine).

Already you may have thought, *Yeah, what you're saying sounds great; but, you don't know about all my responsibilities.* The fact is most of us, to one degree or another, are deceived about what we *have to do,* as was Martha. She was convinced there were many things that had to be done; however, from God's perspective, there were only a few.

Any time we try, on our own, to figure out what God expects of us, look out! We're probably way off. We might decide God expects almost nothing of us, or, on the other hand, we might draw up a list of things that is completely overwhelming. If Satan cannot convince us that God expects nothing out of us, then he will tell us that God expects us to be doing something every minute. In either case, Satan's purpose is to keep us, like Martha, from developing a personal relationship with Jesus Christ. The only way we can gain a true perspective about who we are and what we should be doing is by sitting at His feet and listening to His Word.

I have found this to be true in my personal walk with the Lord, and also in my ministry. As a pastor, I have, on numerous occasions, taken my desires and my plans for the church and surrendered them to God. For example, several years ago a committee was appointed to study the feasibility of buying some property and relocating our downtown church. After an intensive period of study and exploration, a beautiful piece of property on the interstate was located. The night came for the committee's presentation to the church. Everyone was very excited. Just before the committee walked out, one of its members declared he could not go along with the committee's recommendation. We suddenly went from being unanimous as a committee to being divided on the motion. We paused for a moment, prayed for God's guidance, regained our composure, and decided to proceed with the recommendation.

At the church meeting, an intensive and lengthy period of discussion ensued. Charges were made about the committee's motives—and even character! People, whom we thought stood with us, both inside and outside the church, blind-sided us with some misinformation. This caused more heat than light to be shed on the situation. The call for a vote finally came. The recommendation was defeated by a narrow margin. Months of hard work went down the drain.

A surprising thing, however, happened to me during my drive home that evening. As I prayed about what had transpired in that meeting, I realized that we had done our best. We had maintained our integrity and presented the facts as we knew them. Although, for a time, my heart had become set on that piece of property, I ultimately wanted God's will for our church to be accomplished. I knew God is sovereign; so, in that car, I let it go. I stopped all the "what ifs" that were going through my mind and trusted the Lord to guide His people. A quiet peace came into my heart. I remember how suprisingly easy it was for me to fall asleep that night.

Truly God did have control over those circumstances; He had something much better in store for our church. Later, another beautiful site became available to us. Instead of twenty-two acres, we were able to purchase, debt free, one hundred and fifty acres! We have found, since relocating, that the original site would have been too small for us to fulfill the vision that God has given our people.

Like Martha, we were initially deceived as we diligently performed our duties as a committee. Had we sat at His feet with yielded hearts instead of feasibility studies would we have ever recommended the original site? God only knows. I do know we grew as a result of that experience, which I am certain pleases God. We learned to wait on Him to formulate the plan and to be less distracted in our work for Him. This is so necessary for us to resist the voice of the deceiver who tempts us at times to be satisfied at doing the status quo and at other times condemns us for not doing more.

SYMPTOM 3: SHE WAS DISORDERED IN HER PRIORITIES

"'Martha, Martha,' the Lord answered, 'you are worried and upset about *many things*, but only one thing is needed. Mary *has chosen what is better*, and it will not be taken away from her'" (Luke 10:41–42, italics mine).

The "many things" about which Martha worried were not necessarily bad. However, without clearly ordered priorities, good works can become the enemy of well-intentioned believers. More than likely, Martha wanted to hear the words of Jesus, but there were many other things that first had to be done. I am sure that's why she was so upset with Mary.

Does this hold true for you? When push comes to shove, what is the first thing cut from your schedule? If you are like most people, it is usually that which is important but not urgent. For example, if deadlines and bottom lines at work grab a person's immediate attention, the usual tendency is to put time with loved ones and even time with God—aside until the crisis has cleared. If you are guilty of living life from one urgency to the next, you may never get around to what truly is important.

Jesus said that Mary had chosen "what is better" and it would not be taken away from her. You may ask, "What *is* better? How should I set priorities for my life?"

First, you should ask yourself: "Over what would I most grieve if lost?" As discussed in chapter 1, often it is only after we come close to losing something or someone dear that we reexamine our priorities and realize what is indeed important. If you want to experience the abundant life, you must first clarify what truly matters to continually live with that awareness.

Second, you should ask yourself: "As years pass, what parts of my life and which of my actions will bring me regret and which will bring me satisfaction?" For Martha, disordered priorities were the source of her future regret as Christ's life came to an end. The day came all too soon when she wished she had sat with Mary.

SYMPTOM 4: SHE WAS DRIVEN BY HER EFFORTS TO PERFORM

"But Martha was distracted by all the preparations that had to be made. She came to him and asked, 'Lord, don't you care that my sister has left me to do the work by myself? Tell her to help me!'" (Luke 10:40).

In this record of Martha's words, there seems to be an implied answer from Jesus: "Yes, Martha, I do care." I can easily imagine Martha's next words. How often I have heard one of my own daughters cry, "Daddy, tell my sister to come help me!" Or "I did it last! It's her turn! *This just isn't fair!*"

So often, what we say is not what we mean. If Martha had asked the real question of her heart, it might have been, "Lord, don't you notice all that I am doing for You?" Martha's priorities were mixed up because she misunderstood what really pleased Jesus. She thought it was more important to serve than sit. Many Christians today, likewise, get caught up with trying to earn the approval of others, forgetting this is of little value in God's economy.

What motivates a Christian should be the desire to do what is pleasing to God. Sensing God's pleasure in what you do comes from knowing that it is what God wants you to do. Second-guessing God's will is not good enough, for you will never have security in your decision making. That kind of confidence comes only from sitting at His feet.

OLD HABITS ARE HARD TO CHANGE

But the chief priests and Pharisees had given orders that if anyone found out where Jesus was, he should report it so that they might arrest him. Six days before the Passover, Jesus arrived at Bethany, where Lazarus lived, whom Jesus had raised from the dead. Here a dinner was given in Jesus' honor. Martha served, while Lazarus was among those reclining at the table with him. Then Mary took about a pint of pure nard, an expensive perfume; she poured it on Jesus' feet and wiped his feet with her hair. And the house was filled with the fragrance of the perfume. (John 11:57–12:3)

This is almost certainly the same event about which Matthew wrote (see Matt. 26:1–7). The woman, in John's account, who broke the alabaster vial of costly perfume was Mary. Martha was a person who got her identity from what she did for the Lord rather than what He had done (or was about to do) for her. Consequently, during one of the last (if not the last) times Jesus was to be with them, Martha was still in the kitchen serving, while Lazarus and Mary, with the rest, sat and listened to His words.

Mary, after sitting and listening to Jesus' words, recognized that this One who was in their presence was worthy of worship and adoration. She responded in a way that probably did not make much sense to the others present, especially Martha. Mary gave her best to the Lord in heartfelt response to His words. This was not an effort on her part to gain His approval; she was driven by a love for God who was to be bodily present with them for only a short while. Mary chose that part which would not be taken away. She would not have to live with regrets for her actions.

Many Christians today are still distracted by their doing, deceived about their duties, directed mistakenly by their priorities, and driven to perform by wrong motivations. Their identity is in what they do for God rather than what He has done for them. Pleasing God should be the thing that motivates a Christian. As seen in these two accounts, it pleased Jesus when His followers sat at His feet listening to His words. For us to please God and gain His perspective on our obligations and priorities, however, we must get some old habits under control.

STEPS TO GETTING YOUR DRIVING HABITS UNDER CONTROL

I suggest three very simple steps to help control those habits that drive us off course.

CHECK YOUR FUEL

When driving, we often get mad and lose our tempers at other drivers who obviously don't know how to drive, yet act like they own the road. In retrospect, however, the cause of our irritation is rarely the driving habits of other people; it is usually our frame of mind when we first buckle our seat belts. What sets us off, so to speak, is only the last "straw that broke the camel's back" (or the modern translation: "the last guy who cut us off"). When we blow a gasket, it is usually not difficult to discover the root cause. We simply need to stop and ask, *What's fueling this fire?*

What fuels your engine? Is it fear of failure? Is it the longing for self-worth and esteem? Is it the desire to acquire more and more

45

things? What is your fuel's quality? On gasoline pumps there is an octane rating. The higher the rating, the better the quality of gasoline. Are your motivations for driving in your present direction 87 percent pure or would your rating fall even further below God's perfect standard? Significance, esteem, and success, like vapors of gasoline, evaporate quickly.

Last year I attended the annual Prayer Breakfast in Washington, D.C. There I witnessed a strange sight. After the breakfast, the presidential motorcade began to form. I went outside the hotel to watch. There were limousines, Secret Service agents talking into their lapel buttons, scores of motorcycle policemen, and SWAT team sharpshooters on the rooftops. I was fascinated as I watched the president's limo speed away. I guess people in Washington are used to such interruptions because immediately things returned to normal. As I was going back inside, I looked over and saw Andrew Young, the former ambassador to the United Nations, standing all alone, only a few feet from me. Seconds later James Baker, former Secretary of State in the Bush administration, strolled past without anyone noticing. I thought, *A few years ago they were in the parade. Today no one even noticed.*

One day, all of us will walk away from our work, and someone else will take over. I was with a dear friend recently. He had put a great deal of hard work and a huge investment of his life into the institution from which he was about to retire. He said, "A passage from the Book of Ecclesiastes has lately become very personal to me." He referred to Ecclesiastes 2:18–19: "I hated all the things I had toiled for under the sun, because I must leave them to the one who comes after me. And who knows whether he will be a wise man or a fool? Yet he will have control over all the work into which I have poured my effort and skill under the sun."

MAP OUT YOUR COURSE

When my wife, Jeanette, and I go on a trip, I have learned over the years to let her map out our course. Because she is good with details and directions, she handles this task well. I get in the car, get behind the wheel, and then let her navigate. This makes traveling much less stressful for me. There's even an added bonus: if we get lost through some error in her planning or through some navigational mistake, I am not to blame. I just sit back and enjoy the ride.

Jesus did not condemn Martha for working. She was making great time in her drive to get things done, but she was headed in the wrong direction! Many people, driven by the pressures of work or family expectations, find themselves detoured somewhere along the way. They fail to follow God's directions in mapping out life's course.

As I stated before, abundant life for busy Christians is a combination of focusing on high and lofty goals without losing sight of the great things God has already given. It is striving for a feeling of accomplishment while, at the same time, finding true enjoyment in doing what God has called us to do. How can Christians be successful in careers without becoming slaves to their work? We must always remember that "Jesus is the boss" and work for Him and His pleasure.

I remember a line from the movie *Chariots of Fire*. When arguing with his sister about God's plan for his life, Eric Liddell said to her, "Jennie, I feel God's pleasure when I run!" I too have found that when I do God's will, I can work very hard and still feel invigorated because of the sense of God's pleasure in my service. Being driven by the right priorities makes traveling life's journey *almost* as much fun as the anticipated arrival at life's final destination.

OBEY THE RULES OF THE ROAD

Beginning drivers are not allowed behind the wheel until they master some of the essential rules of the road. They are first given a handbook to read. Then they are tested on their head knowledge of that driver's handbook. Once they pass, they must for a period of time, drive with an experienced driver. They are not given a permanent license until they can apply both the written rules and the counsel of experienced drivers to their actual driving experience. After the driver agrees to abide by all driving regulations, the Department of Motor Vehicles then validates and governs the licensing of the driver.

While I was teaching school in Panama City, one of my old fraternity buddies told me to take his new car out for a spin and "try it out—feel the power." Eagerly, I did—right through a quiet neighborhood. That eight-cylinder beauty roared! As I eased my foot off the accelerator, I saw the dreaded flashing blue lights in the rearview mirror. I pulled over. The officer asked for my driver's license and my occupation. I told him I was a school teacher. When I said I was a teacher, he jumped on my case with both feet!

47

"What kind of example are you?" he asked. After chastising me for what seemed an eternity, he told me to "go and sin no more." I may have escaped a fine but certainly not embarrassment!

Christians have been given the "rules of the road" in God's Word, the Bible. These rules should govern their living. The Bible, however, can have no impact on believers' lives until it is read and applied. The true test comes in the living out of God's Word. This is facilitated by the sound teaching of experienced believers. The commitment of believers is only valid if God is the source and the focus of that commitment. All that believers do should be governed by God's presence in their lives.

It is easy to talk Christianity, but putting first things first is the real test of faith. Jesus is the first among all others. The Bible is the first among all books. The Lord's day is the first among all days. The tithe is the first among all expenditures. If a believer gets his or her *firsts* in order, the priorities of life will take order. "Seek first his kingdom and his righteousness, and all these things will be given to you as well" (Matt. 6:33).

Don't let the greatest blessings in life pass you by because you are being driven by an urgent but less important agenda. Don't let a preoccupation with goals and accomplishments cause you to miss out on the most worthwhile and fulfilling way to live your life. We must learn to aim high for great things without losing the ability to live within the moment. We must make sure our priorities are in order. If you flunked the driving test, or if you suffer the symptoms of the Martha Factor, maybe you, too, need to get out of the kitchen before you miss what really matters.

CHAPTER FOUR

OUR PERSPECTIVE OF POSSESSIONS

You hear people talking all the time about their lousy childhoods. They go on to explain why this gave them such a rocky start in life. As I listen to these discussions, I thank God for my childhood and for the great way it launched me into manhood. For the most part, I had a happy childhood. I had many great friends, and we shared a lot of good times. We played hard, worked hard, and got along well. None of us were well-off financially, but that didn't matter. We had gained a sense of security from our parents and in relationship to each other.

THE AMERICAN DREAM

I guess my family would have been categorized as lower middle-class. We definitely were not at the bottom of the economic ladder—I knew people with much less. The truth is, we were happy and secure, for we had an abundance of what really mattered.

When I started junior high school, some things began to take on a different light. I began going to parties, on hayrides, and to dances. There was a girl in my class named Bitsy. I'm sure most of you can remember someone in your class like Bitsy. She was the prettiest, the sweetest, the best-dressed, and the smartest girl in the class. She also had the richest daddy. I remember the first time my

49

friends and I went to a party at (what we called) "Bitsy's Big House." Most of us had never gone to such a huge house with such beautiful furnishings and spacious yard. It was overwhelming. I had seen big, beautiful houses like that before, but I had never known who actually lived in one, at least not well enough to compare myself to them. By Bitsy's standards, we were all poor. It was only then, at her party, when that realization hit me. We had been poor all along, and we didn't even know it.

My perspective on possessions and houses changed again after I was married. I wanted to provide my wife and family a comfortable home in which to live; however, I also tried not to make possessions my number one priority. Fortunately my wife, Jeanette, is a great homemaker. Even when we had far less materially than we do today, she made our home look beautiful—like a castle. She simply has a knack for decorating. Jeanette can undertake huge redecorating projects if the mood strikes. There have been times when I was afraid to get up in the middle of the night for fear she had rearranged the room while I slept!

Three years ago she undertook one of those projects. We had been discussing the need to do some work around the house—a new coat of paint and some recarpeting. I'm sure you know what that means! New paint calls for complementary draperies and offsetting wallpaper. Drapes and wallpaper call for recovering furniture and new pieces of furniture to replace the "uncoverable." New furniture calls for new knickknacks and paintings. New knickknacks and paintings call for new floral arrangements. Oh, I forgot the carpet! New carpet calls for more new carpet. And on it went. Yet Jeanette was amazing. She literally tore our house apart and put it back together in a couple of weeks. (Of course, she was highly motivated. We had her large Bible study class coming to our home for a Christmas party the very week, in fact, the very day after the redecorating was completed. That always seems to work for her.)

After a successful party in our beautiful, but livable, home, Jeanette sat down to rest and to savor the moment over a cup of coffee. She was thinking to herself how pleased she was with her redecorating project. She finally had everything in the house just like she wanted. As she was thinking these things, she picked up her favorite magazine (she had not had time in the last month to stop and look at it). It was a copy of *Architectural Digest*. As she opened its pages, she realized that compared to the houses in that digest our house was not perfectly decorated. In fact, many other homes in that digest came closer to being her dream house than ours did. Her satisfaction turned sour. That's when I entered the room.

"Hi, Babe, how ya doin'?" I said as I bent down to get a big kiss. Instead, I got a big surprise.

"Not so great," she matter-of-factly replied. "I've been looking at this magazine, and I think we've got a long way to go on our house. We need to get started before the relatives arrive for Christmas!"

It seems like our dreams constantly change. In *Whatever Happened to the American Dream,* Larry Burkett says the following:

> When I grew up in the fifties, the American Dream could be defined rather simply: if you work hard and get an education, realistically you can expect to live better than your parents did.
>
> This dream was expanded in the sixties to include a nice home, a nice car, a good education for the children, and retirement at 65, with a reasonable degree of comfort.
>
> In the seventies, the American Dream expanded to include a bigger home, two cars, longer vacations, guaranteed employment, and government aid in everything from housing to health care.
>
> By the eighties the Dream had begun to fade, as the side effects of welfare, drugs, and the "me" generation surfaced. But rather than allow the dream to die, Americans borrowed their way back into prosperity.[1]

Now we're well into the nineties—in fact, we're anticipating the turn of a new century. This is the first generation of Americans who, by and large, do not expect their children to live better and be more prosperous than themselves. It's not that there won't be hundreds of inventions and innovations. In the next ten to twenty years there will be, I'm sure, incredible technological advancements beyond anything presently imaginable. None of this advancement, however, assures that this generation or the next will enjoy a better life or will feel that they finally have enough.

The American Dream is just that, a dream. It is illusive. The dreamer always seems to awaken before possessing the dream. "To have it all" today takes a lot more than it did a few years ago, and it'll take even more in the years to come. It is becoming more and more expensive to be an average American. The stress involved with keeping up with the Joneses is enormous. Many have accumulated a huge mountain of debt trying to do so. It's not going to get any easier in the years ahead either.

In the future there will be more gadgets with which to play, but, at the same time, more symbols of success to maintain. It

51

seems that the more "stuff" there is to have and the more that this "stuff" becomes a part of daily life, the more this "stuff" becomes a perceived need. Many American families now "need" two cars, cable or satellite television, a computer capable of a moon-launch, a cell phone, a microwave oven, voice mail, and an address on the Internet to "get by."

"AND THE PURSUIT OF HAPPINESS"

Americans have pursued happiness with relentless determination and, also, with more success than any other people in history. One of the bedrock ideas on which we established our separate and sovereign nation was the belief that we all possess a God-given right to life, liberty, and the *pursuit of happiness.*

Since the end of World War II, we have achieved unparalleled prosperity and economic growth. In the process, however, we have lost something, and people are desperately looking around to rediscover it, even though they are not exactly sure for what they are searching.

Baby boomers are on the front lines as we press ahead into a new age of anxiety. Part of that anxiety is due to the fact that just as the post-World War II boomers were being born, we as a nation were in the beginning stages of losing touch with God. The war was over, and we were on top of the hill. America had established itself as the greatest and most powerful nation on earth. There had never been such a period of unbridled enthusiasm about future possibilities. Yet, in the years that followed, America made prosperity, growth, and personal happiness the idols by which every other thing was measured (even ourselves) and which everything else served.

Over the last forty to fifty years there has been an ongoing revolution in our expectations. Our parents and grandparents who lived through two world wars, and a depression in between, certainly had a different perspective on happiness. In the fifties, a man would come home from his boring job, wave at the neighbor, cut the grass, try to fix the latest thing that had broken down, watch a little black-and-white TV, and go to bed. Was he any happier than people today? Probably not—but he didn't expect to be. That was life and everyone lived with it. They were more content because what we might consider boring was for them more than their parents had and, often, more than they ever expected.

My expectations were different in those days. Jeanette and I lived in Panama City where I worked as a school teacher. I earned about three hundred dollars a month, and I was glad to earn that. Don't get me wrong. I definitely wanted to move up financially, but in a leisurely way. We were happy with our lives.

Times have changed in our world. Somewhere along the way our expectations of happiness greatly increased. Part of the pain and anxiety people experience today comes from the constant awareness of whether, at any given moment, they are or are not happy. With each new generation that comes along, there is a growing expectation of happiness as a fundamental right and privilege. Many have mistakenly interpreted the idea that we were created equal with the right to pursue happiness as a guaranteed right to constant happiness and instant financial success.

For centuries, people had an understanding of and a belief in two worlds. This present world was a fallen, imperfect, violent place where they must live before going to the better of the two worlds. Complete happiness would only be realized in the next world—in heaven. Ours is in the first (and, perhaps, the beginning of the second) generation of humankind that has expected more happiness in this life than in the next. If you think this lifetime is your only chance for happiness, it is very depressing when you don't have it.

An old commercial used to say, "You only go around once in life. Go for the gusto!" The expectation of rewards in this life even shows up in the theology of some Christians; they seem to believe financial prosperity is the sure sign of faith and godliness. That kind of thinking is an example of how much pagan culture, and, in particular, idolatry in the form of mammon worship, can worm its way into the church.

It is a terrible thing when a generation of people collectively loses touch with God. That does not mean each person in the group has turned away. It means, instead, when God is no longer honored or even acknowledged by the group as a whole, then that generation gradually becomes anti-god, or *atheistic*. Its values and worldview become hostile to those who still believe, who continually fight the beliefs of the ungodly.

IDOLATRY IN AMERICA

Don Richardson, in his book *Eternity in Their Hearts*,[2] points out that most pagan cultures which are today's idol worshipers have at some point in their history worshiped the one true God, the eternal Creator. At some point they turned away from God to worship idols and eventually forgot what had been revealed to them about God. As a result, their great cultures declined morally, spiritually, economically, and educationally. They were judged by God for rejecting the truth that was made known to them. As a result, everything about their culture deteriorated.

Paul understood this. He spoke of the coming judgment of God as a result of people's turning from revealed truth to idols. "The wrath of God is being revealed . . . since what may be known about God is plain to them . . . . For although they knew God, they neither glorified him as God nor gave thanks to him, . . . They became fools and exchanged the glory of the immortal God for images made to look like mortal man and birds and animals and reptiles. Therefore God gave them over in the sinful desires of their hearts" (Rom. 1:18–24).

The idols to which Paul refers in the first chapter of Romans are ancient pagan statues that people worshiped. Yet an idol does not necessarily have to be a statue before which people bow down, burn incense, and offer sacrifices. In the New Testament, Paul refers to covetousness of material possessions as a form of idolatry. "Put to death, therefore, whatever belongs to your earthly nature: sexual immorality, impurity, lust, evil desires and greed, which is idolatry" (Col. 3:5).

If there is an idol in America, what else can it be other than mammon—materialism, affluence, and prosperity? Cars, houses, boats, clothes, jewelry, and club memberships are contemporary symbols of a person's relative worth. Consequently, people derive their perceived value and self-identity from their possessions. Jesus said, "'Watch out! Be on your guard against all kinds of greed; a man's life does not consist in the abundance of his possessions'" (Luke 12:15). Many people live their whole lives with money and material possessions as the highest priorities. Prosperity itself is not bad; we err in the relative importance we place upon it.

Idolatry not only separates us from the peace of God because of its built-in sinfulness, but our idol demands our time and energies. It drains the life from us, keeping us from seeing and remembering what is truly valuable. Not only does idolatry send us off in the wrong direction in search of meaning and contentment, but it morally separates us from the true source of abundant life.

AN UNHOLY ALLIANCE

There is a story in the Bible about two people, Ahab and Jezebel, who made materialism their idol. A little background on these two might be helpful. Ahab reigned twenty-two years as the seventh king of the northern kingdom of Israel. Politically he was one of the strongest kings of Israel. During his reign, Israel was at peace with the southern kingdom of Judah and maintained her dominion over Moab (which paid Israel a considerable tribute).

Ahab's marriage to a foreigner, Jezebel, daughter of the king of the Sidonians, was politically and economically beneficial. Politically, it removed any military threat from Phoenicia. Economically, it brought desired goods to Israel and opened the way for expanded sea trade. Religiously, however, it was disastrous.

Ahab is remembered not for his political or economic advancements, but rather for his religious apostasy. It is said of him, "Ahab son of Omri did more evil in the eyes of the LORD than any of those before him" (1 Kings 16:30). Jezebel introduced the idolatrous worship of Baal to Israel as well as the drunken orgies of the goddess Asherah. Apparently, Ahab worshiped the God of Israel, but probably along with several of Jezebel's pagan deities. He frequently consulted prophets, but the influence of Jezebel overshadowed anything they had to say. Jezebel also instituted a severe persecution against the followers of the Lord, killing all the prophets except one hundred who were hidden by Obadiah.

Ahab's religious corruption was surpassed only by his love of (and display of) material wealth. According to 1 Kings 22:39, he built a palace out of ivory for Jezebel. Ahab's greed, urged on by the idolatrous Jezebel, serves as an example of what happens to many people today. This is shown most clearly in the story of Ahab, Jezebel, and Naboth.

Naboth owned a vineyard that happened to be right next to King Ahab's palace in Jezreel. Ahab wanted the vineyard so that he could, perhaps, make a vegetable garden of it, but Naboth was unwilling to trade or sell at any price. The land, apparently a part of Naboth's family for generations, had been an inheritance. Ahab was depressed, "sullen and angry," the Bible says, so he went home to Samaria to sulk. There he lay on his bed and childishly refused to eat.

Finally, Jezebel, not being one to sit by quietly, demanded to know what was the matter. She said to her emotionally inferior husband, "'Is this how you act as king over Israel? Get up and eat! Cheer up. I'll get you the vineyard of Naboth the Jezreelite'" (1 Kings 21:7). This manipulative woman then wrote letters in the name of Ahab, sealed them with the king's royal seal, and sent them to all the elders and nobles of Naboth's city, Jezreel. In those letters she proclaimed a day of fasting—as if a disaster threatened their town and they needed to humble themselves in the sight of God to avoid His judgment. She then made arrangements for two worthless men to falsely accuse Naboth of cursing God. Her ploy was successful, and, as a result, Naboth was stoned to death. Jezebel wasted no time in telling Ahab of Naboth's execution. At her prompting, he took possession of the vineyard.

If it is true that Satan seeks to draw us to him by tempting us in our weakest area, then the weak area in Ahab's life, which Satan or Jezebel could always exploit, was his covetousness. Jezebel said to him, "Ahab, you deserve to have that field, and I'll make a way for you to get it." Isn't this the same thing we hear every day? We "deserve a break" today. We should "acquire" this or that, and, of course, there's always a way to do it with no money down and no payments until next year.

One of the earliest lessons in being pressured to buy something by a persuasive sales pitch was when I was a six-year-old boy. My uncle took me to the circus in Nashville. While we were seated in the stands, a man came through selling Cracker Jacks. He said that we must buy a box that instant because we might find a valuable prize, perhaps a diamond ring, in the box. That got my attention! I began to clamor for my Uncle B.G. to get me a box of Cracker Jacks. I *had* to have a box of Cracker Jacks!

Uncle B.G. informed me that it was a "rip-off," but that didn't quell my desire for the Cracker Jacks. I insisted until he reluctantly gave into my begging and bought me a box. Boy, I tore into that box, wanting the prize more than the snack. When I finally dug down to my prize (which I anticipated being something akin to the Hope Diamond), I discovered only a dinky plastic toy. As I opened the package in which it was wrapped and looked at it, I turned to my uncle and disappointedly asked, "Is this what you mean by a *rip-off?*" Unfortunately, that's the case all too frequently. The world and its illusions are nothing more than a rip-off.

What has provided Americans such success and so many conveniences is the fact that we live in a free-market economy. It is a system driven by the demands of the consumer. If we provide something that everyone wants, we can be rich.

A necessary part of our market economy is commercial advertising. It is designed to convince us that we want and need a company's product, whether it's really true. Much of it is ridiculous. Advertisers tells us, for example, that if we use a particular brand of toothpaste, it will make us more sexy. If we choose a certain car, it will bring us more friends. If we wear a certain brand of sportswear, it make us better athletes. Well, I tried two out of three, and I can't dunk like Michael Jordan and I am not any sexier! Where's truth in advertising? By it's very nature, marketing techniques tend to be deceptive and breed discontent.

This constant temptation to envy and to covet is becoming the mark of American society. Just as Jezebel tempted Ahab to covet Naboth's vineyard, that same form of temptation bombards our minds every day.

Ahab got his vineyard, but it cost him more than that for which he bargained. The biblical account reads, "There was never a man like Ahab, who sold himself to do evil in the eyes of the LORD, urged on by Jezebel his wife" (1 Kings 21:25).

FOUR WAYS TO KEEP FROM GOING UNDER

Does the way we deal with material possessions really affect our spiritual life? You bet it does! As Jesus taught in the Parable of the Sower, "But the worries of this life, the deceitfulness of wealth and the desires for other things come in and choke the word, making it unfruitful'" (Mark 4:19).

It is hard for us, as believers, to be fruit-bearing when we are caught up in wealth-possessing. Idolatrous materialism is so woven into the warp and woof of the fabric of our culture, it is hard to function without doing service to it. Nevertheless, here are a few suggestions which may help keep us free from the worship of the god of this age and help us maintain a proper perspective of possessions.

1. IDENTIFY THE THINGS IN LIFE THAT BREED DISCONTENT

Back in the seventies, Linda was a student at Cumberland Baptist College in the mountains of eastern Kentucky. Some of the college students from Cumberland would go up into the mountains to work with children in a government preschool education program. At first the Cumberland students were shocked by the backwardness and almost primitive lifestyle of the people. These were mountain people who seldom associated with the folks in town.

57

Many of the children had never even been to the neighboring small town, much less seen what was out in modern America.

One day the college students wanted to take the kids to town and buy them ice cream cones. They were surprised and thought it cruel when one of the fathers would not let his children go. When asked about his decision, he said he did not want his children to see things in that town that they could not have.

Linda is married now and lives in a nice middle-class suburb. She sees the subtle pressure put on her own children by friends from an upper-class neighborhood near their home.

"I understand that father better," she says. "I think we all see too much, and it makes us constantly want more than we can have."

There are very few people who can afford everything they want. Regardless of how much money is made, the list of wants quickly expands to consume it all. Some people have a habit of recreational window shopping. For instance, they will visit a car dealership and look at a fifty-thousand-dollar car. They may be barely able to pay the rent, but they love that new car smell. They sit in it and dream. They also grow in discontent.

Others go shopping when then are depressed, looking for something new to make them feel better. That's what got Ahab into trouble. In his depression, Ahab decided to do a little window shopping. He looked out his window and decided he wanted another vineyard—Naboth's vineyard. He ignored the cost and got what he thought would cure his depression. Then Ahab, as he was about to take possession of the vineyard, was confronted by Elijah with the tab, a prophecy from God. The message from the Lord was a severe one: "'Have you not murdered a man and seized his property? . . . because you have sold yourself to do evil in the eyes of the LORD, I am going to bring disaster on you'" (1 Kings 21:19–21). Ahab's shopping excursion cost him more than he had bargained for.

How does this relate to you as an individual? Think about those desired possessions that occupy your "want list." How do those things affect your finances, your time, your relationship with others, and most importantly, the Lord? Perhaps you need to quit going to car dealerships, to open houses, or even to the mall. Maybe you need to get rid of the catalogs, turn off the commercials, and stop thinking all the time about what you don't—and, maybe, never will—have. You need to guard your mind and your eyes from the things that only serve to breed your own discontent.

58

2. INVESTIGATE THE PROBLEM WHILE SEEKING A SOLUTION

A congressman went into a restaurant with a group of friends. His loud voice and boisterous manner quickly put him center stage in his party. Growing impatient with the somewhat slow service, he shouted at the waitress to come over to his table and take care of them. She did not respond immediately, but rather took her time in coming to his table.

He addressed her abruptly with the words, "Don't you know who I am? I am Congressman Smith. Do you realize whose table you're serving?"

She looked confidently into his eyes and replied, "Don't you know who I am? I am your waitress. I do not care who you are, but it is important that you know who I am. I will take care of you when I can get to you!"

These two individuals appeared to have different perceptions of what the problem was.

Do you have a problem with materialism? Do you judge others by what they have or do not have? I have heard it said that there are some people who initially judge a church by the types of cars parked on Sunday in its parking lot. These individuals drive up and assess whether or not there are enough late model vehicles to indicate their desired level of affluence and compatibility in a church. Now that I think about it, maybe these are the same people that, when they die, want to be buried in their cars!

Sounds pretty shallow, you may be thinking. *I would never be guilty of such superficial Christianity.* Be careful. The problem of materialism in your life may be subtle. The somewhat over-worked saying, Are you a part of the problem or a part of the solution?, might provide an effective clue in the investigation of the effects of materialism on your life.

First, are you a part of the problem? Look at your checkbook. How do you use the resources which God has provided? Do you return to God His tithe? Do you give beyond the tithe—to the church and to others in need? Are you selfish? Do you flaunt your affluence? Do you look down on those less fortunate than you? Are you never satisfied with more? Are you like the child who owns every conceivable toy and game, yet constantly complains to his parents that he's bored and has nothing with which to play? Sometimes we adults can be as self-absorbed and self-indulgent as children.

Second, are you a part of the solution? Don't misunderstand me. It is not necessarily wrong to have beautiful clothes and nice cars. If, however, you are financially blessed, guard the display of your affluence. A responsible believer does not want one who is less fortunate to stumble because of his or her coveting what the believer possesses and displays. In other words, don't show off because in doing so you may cause others to stumble. Paul wrote to Timothy concerning the wealthier members of the congregation: "Command those who are rich in this present world not to be arrogant nor to put their hope in wealth, which is so uncertain, but to put their hope in God, who richly provides us with everything for our enjoyment. Command them to do good, to be rich in good deeds, and to be generous and willing to share" (1 Tim. 6:17–18).

As a pastor I am encouraged when I see financially successful people use their wealth as a means of helping others. I know many people like this. They view their own success as a gift from God. They have matured personally and spiritually in such a way that they are not driven by a need to put their affluence on display. They are more concerned about seeking and serving God than showing off for people.

3. IMPERSONATE CHRIST IN ALL MATTERS OF LIFE

My first year in college I lived in a fraternity house. I wasn't a member, but there were no other rooms available on campus. I had known some of the fraternity brothers from work at a conference center, so they agreed to let me live there. It didn't take long for me to realize that I was living in a world to which I was not accustomed. I found myself in a setting where many of my peers were from affluent families. So, as not to appear out of place, I worked hard at trying to look as if I had everything they did.

My first problem was my clothing. It was a dead give-away. With some creative trading, I was able to borrow clothes from guys who happened to be about my size. This yielded a fantastic wardrobe. Every day I had a different outfit. I could go for three weeks without wearing the same sweater. Consequently, everyone on campus thought I was wealthy—including my new girlfriend.

I didn't exactly tell her I was rich, but I never quite got around to clarifying the matter either. I guess you might understand why. It all worked very well for a long time, that is, until I finally decided to bring that girl home to meet my parents. Of course, she expected to see a beautiful mansion. When we drove up to that little house on Granada Avenue in Nashville, you should have seen the look on her face.

I was pretty nervous about the visit because this was certainly the true test of our relationship. She didn't dump me; instead, she readily accepted me for who I was. Oh, how liberating it was not to have to put on a show any longer! Not only did she accept me for who I was, but that girl, Jeanette, agreed to marry me—just plain ol' me.

We are each made in the image of God. We are His image-bearers. As Christians, we are called to impersonate (that is, "to assume the character or behavior of another") the One whose name we bear. There's no need to try to look like something or someone that we are not. Our security and self-confidence comes from who we are in Him.

The spending habits and indebtedness of many Americans are driven by their efforts to look more affluent and prosperous than they really are. Their lives are full of success symbols to help them appear rich, powerful, and important. Their appearance is a facade, and to maintain that false image, they become slaves to greed. The truly important aspects of their lives are too often neglected—and all this, sadly, for the sake of appearance.

4. INVEST IN WHAT TRULY MATTERS

If an investment counselor told us of a sure fire investment for us—no risks, only guarantees of high dividends—we would probably jump at the opportunity in a minute. Something in us makes us want to get rich quickly. That is what drives people to pour their dollars into lotteries. Jesus said, "Provide purses for yourselves that will not wear out, a treasure in heaven that will not be exhausted, where no thief comes near and no moth destroys. For where your treasure is, there your heart will be also" (Luke 12:33–34).

As a father of three, I can identify with the first statement, with only a slight variation: provide wallets for yourselves that will never wear out. You who are parents know exactly what I mean! As my children were growing up, there always seemed to be extended hands—toward my wallet. Yet, even as the "Daddy, I need this" and the "Dad, can you give me a few bucks" seemed to mount one on top of the other, I knew I was making investments in lives that were dear to me.

Believe it or not, there is an even better investment than in the financial security of your loved ones. It is one with a far greater yield. It is the one for which Jesus called in the preceding Scripture. This investment has eternal returns. While it will set you up for life—and the life to come—it costs everything you've got. It calls for putting Jesus first and putting selfish desires last. It calls for loving others more than loving possessions.

When I finished college, I taught school. In my classroom of sixth graders, I quickly found out snack time was probably their favorite time of the day. At this time, the children were allowed to go to the cafeteria to buy a treat. There was one girl in my class who came from a particularly poor family. I noticed that often when others were getting something, she was unable to buy anything. I made arrangements to make certain that she got something.

One particular day, we ordered popsicles for our snack. They were the two-sticks kind, several flavors. The children loved them and licked them like dogs lapping water on a hot day. After the refreshments, we hit the books again. After a time I saw something that looked like water dripping on the floor from that little girl's desk. I asked her to come to my desk to see if there were some problem.

"What do you mean?" she asked.

"Well," I said, "I saw water under your desk and it concerned me."

"Oh, no!" she cried out. "That's my popsicle!"

"Why didn't you eat it?" I asked.

"I was saving half of it for my brother." she said, "He's never had a popsicle before."

This apparently was the first time that she had ever had a popsicle too. She didn't know it would melt.

This precious child's treasure melted. Even though her motives were pure and her intentions were the best, this young girl's treasure melted. She could not hold on to it.

So it is with our possessions. We may try to save them for our future or securely invest them, but in the end, these possessions are not the primary treasures we should be accumulating. We must be careful we are not seduced into believing the American Dream is our highest goal. Our perspective must be clear. We must see that no matter how good our intentions are—the desire to provide for loved ones or the desire not to be a burden in our old age—unless God controls our purses and our hearts, there is no true security. Unless He possesses all that we are and all that we have, we wind up with nothing that matters eternally.

CHAPTER FIVE

OUR PERSPECTIVE OF GUILT

A letter written by a young wife and mother arrived a couple of weeks after Mother's Day. In it, the woman (whom I'll call Carrie) wrote that she had not been able to come to church to worship on Mother's Day again this year. When she got up and started getting dressed for church, she began to feel sick to her stomach. Maybe she had eaten breakfast too quickly and it would soon pass. The coming minutes, however, only brought more queasiness and then, an intense headache. Her husband and children were disappointed because they had made reservations at Carrie's favorite restaurant for a special Mother's Day brunch following church. She told the family how pleased she was with their thoughtfulness and that she wanted them to go on with their plans. If she felt better, she would join them at the restaurant.

As her family pulled away in the car to go to church without her, Carrie stood at a window sobbing. What was the matter with her? Why couldn't she put the real source of her pain in the past and move on? She felt like she was going to go crazy if she didn't do something about her life.

It was a full half-hour before her tears subsided. She then forced herself to get in the shower so she might prepare herself to join her family at the restaurant. While showering, Carrie could not turn off the anxiety—or her thoughts. With water beating down her tear-streaked cheeks, Carrie began to sort through her past.

Carrie suddenly stopped the replay, got out of the shower, and dressed. For reasons she wasn't sure of then, she wrote the letter detailing her pain, her past, and her guilt.

HOW DID I GET HERE?

For the first time ever, she shared events which occurred almost fifteen years before, during her freshman year of college. Carrie had fallen in love with a senior who was in one of her elective classes. After dating only a short time, they became sexually intimate. Carrie, a Christian, had always planned to "save herself" until marriage. Somehow Scott persuaded her to share herself with him. The relationship lasted only a few months.

Just before spring break, Scott no longer showed Carrie the attention she had previously enjoyed. He was slow to return her calls and seemed preoccupied with other things when they talked. It was during this time that Carrie found out she was pregnant. She was terrified with the news. *How could she have let this happen? What would she tell Scott? What would her parents and friends say? What was she going to do?*

It wasn't long before Carrie found herself at Scott's dorm. As she unburdened her dilemma on him, he coldly looked into her eyes and told her, with graduation just around the corner, he couldn't handle a kid. She needn't worry, though, he would "do right by her" and pay for an abortion.

Scared, feeling alone and used, Carrie had to do something. Because she didn't know what else to do, she had the abortion. No one ever knew except Scott. Shortly thereafter he was out of her life for good—except for his place in her memories and her guilt.

Life went on. Carrie graduated from college. About a year later, she married a wonderful Christian man, Russ. They had three beautiful children and shared much joy in their marriage. They did not, however, share the knowledge of Carrie's secret. During their brief courtship, Carrie never got around to telling Russ about her abortion. After their marriage, it seemed out of the question. In her great happiness with Russ, she thought that she could bury her past.

On numerous occasions, she had asked God to forgive her, yet she never really felt forgiven. At odd times the pain of her sin and guilt surfaced. She might be cooking supper and, all of a sudden, the tears would inexplicably stream down her face. She might be

64

driving in her car listening to a song on the radio and be hit with a tremendous feeling of anxiety, as if her whole world were suddenly crumbling in on top of her.

The guilt never went away. Neither did the pain.

Now, it was another Mother's Day. The obvious reminders—especially thoughts of her being in church on that day—of her being a horrible mother made her sick. This time she had to tell someone. It was becoming much too hard to bear.

She closed her letter with a comment and a question, "I was raised as a Christian knowing right from wrong and had every conceivable advantage. *How did I get here?"*

Tragically, hers is not an isolated case. Abortion is only one of the sources of guilt that confront ministers and counselors today. Our society and our churches are full of people who are shackled by guilt. It colors their perception of their self-worth and binds them in all relationships.

Not only is guilt a major problem with which we, in the helping professions, have to deal, but it is one with which all Christians must deal—pretty much on a daily basis. It is hard for most of us to accept grace and forgiveness, the essential elements of salvation. Too few Christians are able to release the remembrance of sin and failure. As a result, they know little of the peace God affords in His free gift of healing forgiveness.

GUILT'S COURSE

What is guilt? *Guilt is an individual's response to his consciousness of having violated God's holiness.* As sinners, apart from the redeeming work of Jesus Christ, we are guilt-ridden. "For all have sinned and fall short of the glory of God" (Rom. 3:23). We all fall short of God's perfect standard of holiness and righteousness.[1] Our being far less than perfect has accompanying problems—a big one being our ability, or inability, to handle guilt.

Guilt often takes the ugly form of self-condemnation or blame. Its features are inferiority, anxiety, worry, and fear. It only takes us a moment to look in the mirror and see whether these describe our outlook on life. Not recognizing our guilt can lead to self-destructive behavior.

Bill and Sally seemed to have it all together in their marriage and in their lives. Both were dynamic Christians, serving God faithfully in their local church. Yet when things in their relationship began to change Sally sought counsel. She was concerned about Bill—and about them.

Bill, now in his mid-forties, had begun to adopt some destructive patterns in his life. Anger started to surface in ways and in places as never before. Sally, naturally concerned, pleaded with Bill to give her some answers. Was he unhappy at work? Had somebody hurt him in some way? Were they having problems, maybe financially, about which she had no knowledge? Was he mad at her for some reason? Bill seemed to put up a wall and gave no satisfactory response. Sally was confused and upset.

Other things began to change. Bill began to lose interest in their marriage. He did not respond to Sally in the manner to which she was accustomed. He still was at home, going through all the motions of a devoted husband, but he was not there emotionally. His interest in sex had greatly diminished and was, for all purposes, nonexistent. Sally grew lonely and tired of his rejection.

Having stood all she could stand, Sally begged him to go with her to talk to someone in order to save their marriage. He finally agreed to counseling. They went—together and separately—for weeks. Something unbelievable happened in those sessions. Bill began to unburden the load of guilt and shame that had been gnawing at him for years.

There had been sexual misconduct on his part in the early years of his marriage. He had stopped the pattern of sin soon after it had begun and had prayed for forgiveness, but apparently he never fully accepted God's healing. Neither had he confessed to Sally his violation of their marriage vows. Instead, he carried around all that baggage of unresolved guilt for almost twenty years! Finally in the last year, the weight of this baggage had gotten too great for him to bear alone.

It is amazing how God worked in their situation. When he shared his guilt with Sally, she was hurt, yet she was somewhat relieved it was not a problem of present-day infidelity. She felt she could handle the past if Bill would harbor no more secrets and if he would work with her in restoring the marriage. Their story has a happy ending. With counseling and God's healing forgiveness, their relationship was more than restored; it was better than before. It took on glorious new dimensions of honesty and openness.

In dealing with guilt, we, as individuals, must stop and ask, *How did I get here? What has caused me to experience so much pain?* We need to examine the source of our guilt.

TWO CATEGORIES OF GUILT

We all have had feelings of guilt. These feelings signal something wrong in our lives and are often accompanied by some degree of anguish or remorse. Yet are all guilt feelings equally valid? Should we beat ourselves up over every twinge of guilt?

It is helpful to categorize guilt in two ways: true guilt and false guilt.

TRUE GUILT

True guilt may be defined as guilt which is earned. A person experiencing true guilt is doing something wrong or has done something to violate God's perfect standard. God the Holy Spirit convictingly speaks to the conscience of the violator to effect change in that individual's life.

To those who are embroiled in sin, the voice of the Holy Spirit may not be as discernible as the voice of an irate husband when it boomed over the public address system at a local drive-in movie theater one Saturday night. "My wife is here with another man. Would both parties please report immediately to the concession stand?" Reportedly twenty cars immediately sped from the parking lot. We should be as sensitive to the prompting of the Holy Spirit!

Dr. Earl Wilson, in his book *Counseling and Guilt*, describes two types of true guilt. The first type of true guilt is *active guilt*. It is guilt over ongoing sinful behavior that is unresolved. The Holy Spirit is trying to lead the person to stop the sin, confess, and receive God's forgiveness. The sin may occur again because of the person's weakness and failure to rely on God's strength. The individual, however, should continue to listen to the leading of the Holy Spirit to cease, to confess, and to accept God's forgiveness.

The second type of true guilt may be called *unfinished guilt*. This type of true guilt occurs when sin has been forgiven, yet the person continues to struggle with the sin itself, even though they may not be succumbing to it. Unfinished guilt can also be seen in situations where the sin may have been confessed and forgiveness received, but all the consequences of the sin has not been experienced.[2]

A person who has had a problem with alcohol abuse may continue to experience this type of unfinished guilt months or even years after becoming sober. Guilt may surface as this person is tempted to repeat destructive behavior or it may surface as the person deals with the consequences of alcoholism. At those times,

67

instead of feeling guilty, one should focus instead on feelings of gratitude for what God has already accomplished through forgiveness in his or her life.

True guilt should be looked upon as God's gracious gift. Our Heavenly Father loves us so much He desires to correct us, not destroy us. His gracious use of true guilt has been likened to an engraver's use of acid. When used in small doses, this acid can effectively be used to clean, refine, and perfect His original design.[3] God, through true guilt, gives us another chance to do what really matters in life, instead of that which is sinful and harmful.

FALSE GUILT

The second major category of guilt is false guilt. While true guilt comes from divine judgment and intervention, false guilt comes as a result of the judgments and suggestions of a particular individual.[4] In other words, self, others, and Satan are the sources of my false guilt. This type of guilt is unearned. It is subjective, but, nonetheless, painful. It may take the form of shame when one doesn't feel capable of doing any good in life and may be tied to feelings of inadequacy or failure. It may take the form of dredging up old childhood feelings of naughtiness. This category of false guilt may be classified by its three sources.

1. Imagination. This source of guilt is one with which it is difficult to deal—your imagination. It is difficult in that the thoughts and reasons behind this false guilt are often buried in the chambers of the inner sanctum of your subconscious. This feeling of guilt may be vague and not well defined, or it may be attached to thoughts and actions that are considered forbidden. Teens may struggle with this type of guilt over lustful thoughts concerning the opposite sex. Adults may feel guilty for not achieving their dreams.

The source can also be the shame to which I earlier alluded. It arises when you don't meet your own expectations of what your ideal self should be. You feel guilty by harboring such thoughts as, *If I had more character, I could have handled this situation better* or *I am just not good enough.*

2. Imposition. The second source of false guilt is guilt which is imposed on us by others. This is where individuals allow others to manipulate them and cause them to feel unmerited guilt. We are familiar with the comic example of a mother saying to her child who refuses to eat his vegetables, "You should eat all of your food because there are starving children in Rwanda." To which the child responds, "Name one!" Then there's the classic example of a guy trying to make a girl feel guilty of not loving him enough by saying to her, "If you really love me, you'll go all the way with me." Teammates and coaches also use fake guilt with athletes. They are made to feel guilty if they let the team down by a poor performance. Tragically, when the expectations of parents are not met, children frequently carry around feelings of false guilt for years or even for life.

3. Incrimination. A third source of false guilt is incrimination by Satan. This type of guilt is Satan's favorite tool. The Bible calls him the "the accuser of our brothers" (Rev. 12:10) because Satan is always ready to impose guilt upon the forgiven family of God. While the Holy Spirit's guilt is constructive in the lives of believers, Satan's guilt is totally destructive. Through true guilt the Holy Spirit seeks to draw us closer to God. Through incriminating, false guilt Satan seeks to separate us from God.

Satan likes nothing better than for believers to doubt their forgiveness, their salvation, or their worth as children of God. My heart is often wrenched during conversations with elderly Christians—believers most of their lives—who have been robbed of the joy of their salvation and the assurance of God's forgiveness because Satan's insidious lies have planted doubt and guilt.

SOMETIMES LIFE IS THE PITS

Have you ever asked someone how they were doing and they replied that they were "the pits"? Some years ago Erma Bombeck wrote a book entitled *If Life Is a Bowl of Cherries, What Am I Doing in the Pits?* It was a humorous look at life's challenges. Joseph was a biblical character who could have probably written the definitive book about life "in the pits."

Joseph was eleventh of the twelve sons of Jacob. He was the favored son, the firstborn of Rachel and the son of Jacob's old age. Because of his father's favoritism toward him, Joseph received a coat of many colors—perhaps indicative of Jacob's intention to make Joseph the head of the tribe. Naturally, this made his brothers envious. Also, Joseph's interpretation of two dreams, by which he suggested their future subservience to him, further provoked his brothers.

One day when Joseph went to check on his brothers' flock-tending some distance from home, the brothers saw an opportunity to kill him and make the fulfillment of his dreams impossible. Reuben, however, persuaded them not to kill him, but to throw Joseph alive into a deep pit. Plans changed once again when Joseph's brothers sold him to a caravan of Ishmaelites headed to Egypt.

God was with Joseph in the pit and in Egypt. Joseph was sold in a slave market to Potiphar, an officer of Pharaoh. While a slave to Potiphar, Joseph—because of God's being "with him"—was successful in everything he did (see Gen. 39:2). "Joseph found favor in his eyes and became his attendant. Potiphar put him in charge of his household, and he entrusted to his care everything he owned. From the time he put him in charge of his household and all that he owned, the LORD blessed the household of the Egyptian because of Joseph" (vv.4–5a).

Joseph was a man of integrity and, as such, refused the sexual advances of Potiphar's wife. Spurned, she falsely accused Joseph of attempting to violate her. Joseph was thrown into prison as a result. Again, Joseph, with no guilt of wrongdoing, found himself imprisoned and sold out by those closest to him. Talk about life being the pits!

OH, BROTHER, ARE WE IN TROUBLE NOW

While in prison, Joseph continued to prosper because "the LORD was with him" (Gen. 39:21a). "So the warden put him in charge of all those held in prison, and he was made responsible for all that was done there" (v. 22). Dream interpretation was the means God used to release Joseph from prison. After a set of circumstances and after at least two years in prison, Joseph found favor in the eyes of Pharaoh by interpreting two dreams that no others could interpret. He not only was released from prison, but he was also put in charge of Pharaoh's palace. Not a bad promotion!

Joseph devised a plan to save Egypt from seven years of impending famine. "The plan seemed good to Pharaoh and to all his officials. . . . Then Pharaoh said to Joseph, 'Since God has made all this known to you . . . all my people are to submit to your orders. Only with respect to the throne will I be greater than you'" (Gen. 41:37–40).

Famine hit Egypt and all the surrounding countries as well. "When Jacob learned that there was grain in Egypt, he said to his sons, 'Why do you just keep looking at each other?' He continued, 'I have heard that there is grain in Egypt. Go down there and buy some for us, so that we may live and not die'" (Gen. 42:1–2). Maybe his sons were just looking at each other and not doing anything because of paralyzing guilt. Right after that, Scripture indicates they felt God was punishing them for bringing harm to Joseph (see Gen. 42:21).

The brothers went to Egypt, and, as God ordained, they came face to face with Joseph (although they did not recognize him). It was Joseph to whom they reported to receive an allotment of grain. We soon realize he had turned the matter over to God a long time before that encounter. Although Joseph recognized his brothers, he (incognito) received them with open arms but chose to test them before embracing them. The brothers were forced to face the sin which brought their guilt.

Joseph accomplished this by orchestrating a series of events designed to test his brothers. Their relationships to each other, to their father, and to God had been affected by their guilt. Now these relationships were put on the line to test their strength. Needless to say, the relatively short process was painful. Genesis 42:21 reveals their pain, as well as their guilt: "They said to one another, 'Surely we are being punished because of our brother. We saw how distressed he was when he pleaded with us for his life, but we would not listen; that's why this distress has come upon us.'" Oh, brother, what's next?

WHAT HAS HAPPENED TO ME?

Guilt, like sin, comes with a price tag. It may be a good bargain, as is the case when God intervenes in destructive behavior; or it may be a rip-off, as is Satan's highway robbery of a believer's assurance. Dr. Paul Faulkner suggests that when we violate our moral values, we create a psychological debt which must be paid back, one way or another. Our conscience is the debt collector who stays after us until the debt is satisfied.[5]

Let's explore the cost of guilt and its payment by focusing on guilt's toll on three relationships.

RELATIONSHIP TO OTHERS

We often toss around phrases like "I owe it to him to . . . ," "I am indebted to you for . . . ," or "I'll never be able to repay you." Our language is a dead give-away of our thinking, especially in this area of relationships. We tend to barter our emotional support in friendships and familial relationships. Why do we respond the way we do to others? Although this is a pretty complex question, I

71

would like to offer guilt as a part of the answer. Guilt can play a major role in the way we relate to others.

Guilt may cause us to do things that we otherwise might not do, good or bad, for the person who is pulling our strings. My wife, Jeanette, knows exactly how to pull my strings! She loves antiques. My tendency is to view them as old things somebody else didn't want, yet I have to pay an exorbitant price for the privilege of releasing them from their junk. Through the years she has implored me to go with her to antique shops—a task I find about as exciting as having a root canal. Sometimes she is able to guilt me into going. How can I say no when I think of the many times she sat through rain, cold, and heat for two hours to watch twenty-two guys knock each other down over a piece of leather? She prefers her leather as fine, aged upholstery, and she also prefers not to have to knock anyone down to score a purchase. So I go with her out of a sense of guilt.

It has also been suggested that we have in us a sense of owing a debt which causes us to seek to atone for wrongs done by paying back our debts—often by punishing ourselves. Again, our language reveals this. When a person is released from prison, we say he has paid his debt to society.[6]

The working mother often feels indebted to others for their help in transporting and caring for her children while she is at work. This mom, out of guilt and gratitude, on her times off from work, may try to reconcile the account with the other parents by helping out with their children. This may be a positive aspect of guilt, if one is not too obsessive in the payback.

The negative aspect might be seen in the parent who has wronged his child, perhaps abusively, who seeks, out of guilt, to buy back the affections of his child through excessive gift-giving.

Guilt can destroy relationships with others. Our friends and family members, not knowing or understanding our guilt, can be left in the dark as to why we respond to them in the manner in which we do. Both Carrie's and Bill's stories illustrate this. Their guilt affected their relationships with their loved ones. Guilt can surface in our relationships through anger, and even rage. The guilty party may alienate those whom he or she loves because of the way guilt is expressed in his or her life.

RELATIONSHIP WITH SELF

In the Bible, we find the word *iniquity* used where we might, in non-biblical writing or speech, use the word *sin*. It is used there to indicate sin which is not an isolated problem, but rather a condition of one's being. I like one man's explanation of its use: "Iniquity is used to mean that there is something twisted in me that needs to be straightened out by the grace of God. There is something bent that needs to be unbent; there is something crooked that needs to be straightened out."[7] Sin and its accompanying guilt are like that. There is something inside which must be corrected.

Whether the guilt is true or false guilt, it may have a debilitating effect on the individual—spiritually, psychologically, and physically.[8] This was true in the cases of both Bill and Carrie. The debt of their guilt was being paid in all three areas. This is true of all unresolved guilt. It is probably the most devastating of all emotions.

Unresolved guilt is anxiety producing and demoralizing. It can rob one's life of enjoyment and satisfaction. It can steal one's inner peace and well-being. It can surface in paralyzing fear, denial, depression, and restlessness.

Relief is often sought through all the wrong means of escapism: total devotion to work or a cause, pleasure seeking or reckless abandonment. Sometimes chemicals are used to numb the pain, but the guilt only increases. It is hard for one to escape guilt; it is relentless.

I have often counseled people who have said to me that they cannot live with themselves or that they do not like themselves. It usually doesn't take much inquiry for me to soon discover there is unresolved guilt at the root of their problems. My task is then to help them find the source—or Source—of that guilt.

RELATIONSHIP TO GOD

Unresolved guilt begs us to face God. Until we do, guilt can cause us to blame God for our misery, to avoid God, or to grow indifferent toward Him. Guilt as it is approached in our relationship to God needs to be understood not only as a psychological issue, but also as a theological issue.

As a theological issue, guilt should cause us to examine our sin nature and the nature of a holy and just God. Convicting and true guilt is used by the Holy Spirit to help us realize our hostility toward God as demonstrated by our inclination to sin. How good God is to not leave us to our sinful desires by allowing our consciences to be provoked! As a tool of the Master Designer, true guilt can mold the most unmalleable sinner into the form of an adopted child of righteousness.

73

Weekly, I have the joy of seeing this miracle of God's gracious use of guilt in bringing the lost to a realization of their need for Him. Young and old alike are awakened from the lethargy of their sin by the effective nudge of the Holy Spirit on their sleepy hearts. I was reminded of this when I ran into Sue.

Sue informed me that her husband just celebrated his birthday over the weekend, and the next day was her birthday. It probably wasn't a polite thing to do, but I innocently asked Sue how old she would be. She responded proudly, "I'll be sixty-four tomorrow!" I think I redeemed myself when I told her, in all honesty, that she looked way too young to be older than me. Then, out of curiosity, I asked what birthday it was for Howard. I wasn't prepared for her answer, "One year old!"

It took me a second to realize what she meant. Howard had just celebrated the first anniversary, or birthday, of his being born again as a Christian. What a great day it was, a year ago, when Howard recognized his guilt as a sinner and responded to the free gift of salvation through Jesus Christ!

Upon an invitation to their home, I had dropped by to visit with Howard and Sue. Sue had been praying for years, along with many fellow believers, for Howard's salvation. Howard, who was sixty-seven at the time, had been experiencing some serious health problems. Until this point in his life, he had been indifferent to the things of God. Over the course of the previous nine years, some change had begun to occur in Howard's life as he was developing sensitivity to the things of God. The Lord used Howard's illness to bring fear and guilt, conviction and remorse, over his lifetime of sinful separation from God.

All it took was my talking with him, friend to friend, to gently guide him in making a decision that God already had in the works. What a joy it was to see this man, who was hooked by tubes to an oxygen tank, finally admit his need for spiritual healing, over and above the physical healing he, too, so desperately needed. God answered many of Howard's prayers that day. Not only did God bring spiritual healing in Howard's relationship to Him, but also healing in many strained interpersonal relationships.

Howard, as a husband and a believer, could relate to his beautiful Christian wife in ways they had never experienced in their forty-seven years of marriage. He could now be the father and grandfather God had intended him to be to his children and his grandchildren. God began to heal the scars of wasted opportunity. God also began healing Howard physically. Improved physical health allowed Howard to begin to attend church regularly and to be able to diligently study His Word at home.

"The Bible is the most fascinating book I have ever read," he recently proclaimed. "I can't believe what I was missing all those years by not having a personal relationship with Jesus."

What an unbelievable change God brought into this older man's life!

Initially Howard, like many others, had a false perception of the character of God. God was negatively viewed as a condemning tyrant who enjoys burdening His subjects with a heavy taxation of guilt. Howard carried that assessment of guilt with him for more than six decades before laying his burdens at the feet of a compassionate and forgiving Lord.

A false perception of God and a burden of false guilt can absolutely affect the way we look at what matters in life—especially how we perceive a relationship with God. It is imperative that we rethink the guilt we carry and carefully determine its source.

How Do I Get Out?

When I have gotten myself in a jam, the first thing I have usually attempted to do is to find the means by which to get myself out of the jam. I remember a major jam I got myself into as a boy. Two spinster sisters, both school teachers, lived two doors down from our house in a beautiful white house—a tempting target for homemade mudballs.

One day while the Arledge sisters were gone, my brother Joe and I threw mudballs until the house was covered with brown spots—giving it the appearance of a bad case of measles. We ran away from the scene of our crime and back home where no one would find us out. The guilt we felt was tremendous. Talk about a jam! There seemed no way out.

To our bitter chagrin, the perceptive sisters soon called our parents, and we were brought back to the scene of our mudball assault. We unburdened our guilt upon them, and, compassionately, they accepted our apologies. Yes, we had to clean up the crime scene and wash away all evidence of our mudball onslaught. Then something amazing happened. The kind sisters extended an open invitation for us to come back to their home again—any time—with no need of feeling guilty for what was in the past. It felt so liberating to get out of that jam.

When in a jam with guilt and sin, our conscience implores us to do something to get us out of the jam. Freedom from guilt is the sweetest of all freedoms, but independence is not its liberating cry. Rather, independence may be exactly what got us in the jam to begin with. Dependence on God is our only true liberation from guilt.

Remember our friend Carrie? We left her story as she was sending out a cry for help. The good news is she received that help. Her letter brought the pastoral response she needed to feel some reassurance that she really was loved by God and that God was able to forgive her sin. For the special help she needed, Carrie was confidentially brought to a post-abortion support group.

There she drew comfort from knowing that she was not alone in her struggle. Most women in the group were Christians who, like her, made a costly error. They, too, struggled with relentless guilt. They felt shame and feared they might be found out by their families, their friends, and their community of believers.

Eventually Carrie was able to let go of the guilt that she had held for so many years. She discovered her sin was against God, and He certainly was a big enough God to be able to forgive her. She felt healed and totally transparent before Him. Only then was she able to face her husband. For her healing to be complete, she felt she needed to be transparent before him.

With her counselor's assistance, Carrie shared her years of guilt and shame with Russ. He had not had a clue as to what was bothering her for so long, but he knew that she harbored some sort of pain. He expressed his unconditional love—and the forgiveness she sought—with little hesitation. He loved her and wanted all of her back in his life. Carrie was well on the road of healing in her relationships.

TWO AVENUES OUT OF THE PIT

FIRST AVENUE: EASY STREET

Sometimes the easiest way out is not the best route to take. Such is the case with guilt. Too often we try the easiest means of escape from the prison of our guilt. There are four landmarks that help us know if we are heading in the wrong direction.

The first landmark we pass is the one where we try to *ignore* our guilt. We try to pretend that there is no guilt present in our lives. We don't face our troubled consciences. Often this allows us to repeat patterns of sin, for we assume no responsibility in facing our sin.

The second landmark we pass is the one where we try to *deny* our guilt. As the guilt keeps surfacing, we keep refusing to deal with it. We say to ourselves that we don't really have a guilt problem.

The third landmark we pass is the one where we try to *hide* our guilt. We carefully mask, as best we can, all symptoms. We pretend to be someone we are not.

The fourth landmark we pass is the one where we try to *transfer* our guilt. This is easy to do in the present age of outspoken victimization. Pass-the-buck-ism is another way to look at this path of dealing with our guilt. Years ago, as the character *Geraldine*, Flip Wilson would comically retort, as he did something he should not, "The devil made me do it!" We, too, transfer blame instead of facing up to our debt of guilt.

SECOND AVENUE: THE HIGH ROAD

When traveling in Israel, I am always impressed by the road up the face of Masada, the site of the Jews' last stand against the Romans in A.D. 70. Masada occupies the top of a huge mesa near the southeastern coast of the Dead Sea. On it are the fascinating remains of Herod the Great's palace and fortifications. The height of the fortress, the angle of ascent, and the oppressive heat of the region make the journey up the face of the mesa difficult, to say the least. That was the idea when the Jews were trying to make it impregnable to enemy's attack. (They certainly didn't have tourists in mind in those days.)

While I have hiked *down* the face of Masada, I have always chosen to take the cable car *up* or traveled an easier trail up the back. In my descent down the face of the mesa, I was constantly aware of my need for sure footing and the need to stay on the pathway. Our avenue to forgiveness and the healing of guilt is a lot like that path up Masada. It is not without risk, and it requires carefully following God's prescribed way.

With the blood of His Son, Jesus Christ, God has paved the way for us to get on top of our guilt. To accept what God has already accomplished for us, there are spiritual and practical things we must do. I have adapted some biblical and psychological principles outlined by Dr. Larry Crabb[9] which provide an excellent model for us, as Christians, to follow.

77

1. Identify guilt feelings

2. Identify guilt behavior

3. Identify guilt thinking

4. Clarify biblical thinking

5. Commit to dealing with guilt problem

6. Plan and carry out biblical behavior

7. Identify Spirit-controlled feelings

I believe the true avenue to our relinquishing guilt's hold on our lives is for us to recognize only God can remove the guilt and heal our consciences. This is what God did for Joseph's brothers.

For years they had, undoubtedly, been tormented by guilt. Now God, who was *with* Joseph, used Joseph to force his brothers to bring the youngest brother, Benjamin, and their father, Jacob, to Egypt. Having everyone assembled in one place allowed God to confront the brothers with their guilt and make them transparent before all concerned parties. Only then, could healing in their lives begin.

To gently effect healing, Joseph first revealed his identity to his brothers before Jacob's arrival in Egypt.

> So there was no one with Joseph when he made himself known to his brothers. And he wept so loudly that the Egyptians heard him, and Pharaoh's household heard about it. . . . [His brothers] were terrified at his presence. Then Joseph said to his brothers, "Come close to me." When they had done so, he said, "I am your brother Joseph, the one you sold into Egypt! And now, do not be distressed and do not be angry with yourselves for selling me here, because it was to save lives that God sent me ahead of you. For two years now there has been famine in the land, and for the next five years there will not be plowing and reaping. But God sent me ahead of you to preserve for you a remnant on earth and to save your lives by a great deliverance. So then, it was not you who sent me here, but God. He made me father to Pharaoh, lord of his entire household and ruler of all Egypt." (Gen. 45:1b–8)

Joseph showed keen, mature insight in restoring relationships through unconditional love and forgiveness. Obviously, God was in control of his life and had healed old wounds many years prior. Now God used Joseph to do the same in the lives of his brothers.

We are told that Joseph "kissed all his brothers and wept over them. Afterward his brothers talked with him" (v. 15). The Bible does not record the brothers' words when Joseph revealed himself to them. It doesn't say anything about them making excuses for what they did. Maybe they felt so secure in Joseph's explanation and forgiveness that they were able to immediately enjoy God's cleansing of their guilt.

Joseph—who, in many ways, foreshadows Jesus—continued to facilitate God's work in the lives of his brothers by sending them to their father and having them confess their guilt and sin. The brothers returned to Egypt with Jacob, where they were reconciled by the work of their brother, whom they had tried to kill, before their father. The brothers were then received as heirs to the kingdom, assuming their places in the family of the ruler, with all privileges and blessings. "So Joseph settled his father and his brothers in Egypt and gave them property in the best part of the land, the district of Rameses" (Gen. 47:11). Not only did his brothers receive "the best of the land of Egypt," they were allowed to live off "the fat of the land" (Gen. 45:18), having their every need met through their brother.

God is so good to allow insight into how He worked through guilt and forgiveness in the lives of Joseph's family. His preservation of their story gives each of us hope that He can and will do the same for us.

HOW DO I STAY OUT?

A young wife asked her husband, "Honey, why don't you tell me you love me any more?" He insensitively responded, "I told you once that I loved you, and if I ever change my mind, I'll let you know." Most of us, like that young wife, want reassurance—in relationships, in job performance, in school grades, and also in forgiveness.

We may have head knowledge about being forgiven, but somehow, we just don't *feel* forgiven. This is where a personal and abiding relationship with Christ can help. The greater our intimacy with the Lord, the lesser our insecurities. The more time we spend getting to know the Person and character of God the Son, the more we will be able to trust what He has accomplished for us.

The Bible speaks of our *knowing* God in the same terms it uses to describe sexual knowledge of a marriage partner. The intimacy we share with the Lord should grow over the years, like the intimacy shared in the marriage relationship. If we are not growing closer to the Lord, chances are we are growing away from Him. We need to guard our union with Him and continue to grow in relationship with Him.

My marriage is like that. I married my college sweetheart, Jeanette. I couldn't wait to get to know her better! I greatly enjoyed the intimacy of our early months and years of marriage. I felt secure in her love and her desire to have me as her husband. Yet our lives did not remain the same as the day we said our "I do's." Work and family obligations constantly demanded more of our time and energy.

This is where a lot of marriages get in trouble; however, this is where ours grew even more solid. With greater demands on my time, I needed someone on whom I could lean. Jeanette is that perfect support for me. Her strengths ideally complement my weaknesses. I have grown in my deep appreciation of her constant loving care and devotion to me.

I have also grown in my attraction to her as she has become more beautiful over the years—physically and spiritually. I believe as she grows in her mature relationship with the Lord, the lovelier she becomes. I can see His goodness on her face and in her eyes. I am drawn to her great inward and outward beauty.

Yes, I still love her hugs and kisses! She is the most desirable woman I know. She makes me feel like the man of her dreams (no, not nightmares!).

Today, after thirty-six years of marriage, I am more secure in Jeanette's love than ever. I have every assurance our marriage will last "till death do us part."

This was not the case with Joseph's brothers. They felt pretty good about things as long as their daddy was alive. Maybe they thought Joseph was being nice to them on Jacob's account. When Jacob died, however, they were afraid of retribution by Joseph, and said, "'What if Joseph holds a grudge against us and pays us back for all the wrongs we did to him?'" (Gen. 50:15b). They sent Joseph instructions given by Jacob before he died: "'I ask you to forgive your brothers the sins and wrongs they committed in treating you so badly. Now please forgive the sins of the servants of the God of your father.'" When their message came to him, Joseph wept. His brothers then came and threw themselves down before him. "We are your slaves," they said (vv. 16–18).

Again we see in Joseph a foreshadowing of Jesus when he reassured them their forgiveness had already been accomplished and they need not fear further punishment for their sins. Somehow, in their time already spent in Egypt, they had not availed themselves of the opportunity to grow closer to the brother who was now their savior. They were too insecure to know how much he loved them and how, with God, he had completely forgiven them. "But Joseph said to them, 'Don't be afraid. Am I in the place of God? You intended to harm me, but God intended it for good to accomplish what is now being done, the saving of many lives. So then, don't be afraid. I will provide for you and your children.' And he reassured them and spoke kindly to them" (vv. 19–21).

We are not told through the Scriptures if they ever really grew closer as brothers or if they ever enjoyed the assurance of their forgiveness. We don't know if guilt plagued them for the rest of their lives. They do make us stop and think, however, about our own dealings with guilt and forgiveness.

An old hymn reiterates the blessedness of knowing forgiveness—especially the forgiveness of God:

Blessed assurance, Jesus is mine!
Oh, what a foretaste of glory divine!
Heir of salvation, purchase of God;
Born of His Spirit, wash'd in His blood.[10]

How can we get out and stay out of the pits of life? We must change our perspective. Satan must not distort the way we look at the important matter of guilt. We must stay away from those things which bind us and cast us into the pit. We then must grow closer to the only One who can keep us from future bondage to guilt and shame—the almighty, all-loving, all-forgiving God.

PART TWO

FOCUSING OUR PERSPECTIVE

CHAPTER SIX

OUR PERSPECTIVE OF FAITH

Franz-Josef I of Austria, a member of the Hapsburg dynasty and the last great emperor of Europe, died in 1916. His was the last of the extravagant imperial funerals. The long funeral procession of dignitaries and elegantly dressed court personages escorted the coffin, draped in the imperial colors of black and gold. With the military band playing the funeral dirge and with torches lighting the way, they marched with the body of Franz-Josef through the streets of Vienna and descended the stairs of the Capucin Monastery. At the bottom was a great iron door which guarded the Hapsburg family crypt. Behind the door was the Cardinal-Archbishop of Vienna.

The officer in charge followed the prescribed ceremony, established centuries before.

"Open!" he cried.

"Who goes there?" responded the Cardinal.

"We bear the remains of His Imperial and Apostolic Majesty, Franz-Josef I, by the Grace of God Emperor of Austria, King of Hungary, Defender of the Faith, Prince of Bohemia-Moravia, Grand Duke of Lombardy, Venezia, Styrgia . . . ." The officer continued until he had finished listing the emperor's thirty-seven titles.

"We know him not," the Cardinal replied. "Who goes there?" The officer spoke again, but this time using a much abbreviated and less ostentatious title reserved for times of expediency.

"We know him not," the Cardinal said again. "Who goes there?"

85

The officer tried a third time, stripping the emperor of all but the humblest of titles: "We bear the body of Franz-Josef, our brother, a sinner like us all!"

At that the doors swung open, and Franz-Josef was admitted.[1]

Death is the great equalizer. In death there are no titles, no dynasties, no fame, and no wealth so impressive or so worthy as to open the doors of salvation. Only those who humbly acknowledge their position as sinners and their need of a Savior can enter the kingdom of God.

THE ONLY KEY TO THE KINGDOM

Have you ever locked yourself out of your car or your house? It certainly can make you feel foolish—especially when it's your fault. Actually, you don't feel much better when it's someone else's fault. I recall an incident which occurred a few years ago. My wife and I were catching a plane out of Nashville to Orlando. The airlines had over-booked the flight and offered to give a free flight to any U.S. destination for those willing to catch a later flight. Jeanette seized the opportunity, stayed behind, and caught a later flight. Because of church commitments, I needed to get back to Orlando at the scheduled time, so I flew back without her—and without any keys.

I didn't drive myself home after my flight landed, so it wasn't until I got home and reached for my keys that I discovered I had none. It was late, and I didn't want to disturb anyone, so I futilely looked for a way inside: an unlocked door or window. The house was securely locked up. I had to go next door, disturb our neighbors, and see if they still had a key to our house. They had the key I needed. I was able to get inside my home.

The thing is, when we're locked out, people with the wrong keys are of no true help. They might have rings of keys which look like they fit our need, and they might even make us feel better by sharing their support and understanding; but the truth is, they can't help us gain entrance where we need to be. It's much the same when we can't seem to get where we want to be going in life.

We may feel locked out from the things that really matter in life, and we can't seem to find the right key to gain entrance. We may have tried the keys and suggestions offered by many others, but none fit our true need. There are motivational books by the scores with such titles as *The Keys to Happiness, The Keys to Success,* and

The Keys to a Better Life. When these keys don't seem to fit, we look for another and another. Yet there is only one key that fits.

Jesus said, "'I am the First and the Last. I am the Living One; I was dead, and behold I am alive for ever and ever! And I hold the keys of death and Hades'" (Rev. 1:17b–18). He also said "'I am the way and the truth and the life. No one comes to the Father except through me'" (John 14:6). Now these are keys that fit every situation. Jesus holds some amazing keys—the keys to life and death. In fact, He *is* the key to abundant life.

Abundant life comes from knowing Jesus Christ. "In him was life," John's Gospel says, "and that life was the light of men. The light shines in the darkness, but the darkness has not understood it" (John 1:4–5). The Greek word *katalambano*, translated in this verse as "understood," has two meanings. One meaning is "to overtake" or "to take away." It can also be translated "to perceive" or "to comprehend." Either meaning provides an important key to our understanding of the abundant life and light Christ has brought to a dark world.

First of all, the darkness cannot *take away* the light. I like the lyrics of the children's song, "This Little Light of Mine": "I've got something that the world can't give, and the world can't take it away." Children sometimes sing, "Don't let the devil blow it out." The true Light of life cannot be extinguished. The world tried its best to eradicate the man Jesus Christ, but death could not extinguish His light—for He held the keys to death and life!

Second, people who live in darkness seek light, but even when many look directly at the Source of light and life, they don't *recognize* it. It would be like looking straight up in the sky at noon on a clear day in sunny Florida and not seeing the sun. You would have to be blind. So it is with many people—especially prideful and self-made people.

The self-righteous, hypocritical, religious leaders tried to entrap Jesus by having Him pass judgment on a situation involving a woman caught in adultery. Their plan was foiled when He put the burden of judgment back on their shoulders. They quickly left the scene after they failed to extinguish the flame of righteousness that burned brightly in Jesus and pierced holes in the darkness that enveloped them.

Christ explained His role to the adulterous woman by saying, "'I am the light of the world. Whoever follows me will never walk in darkness, but will have the light of life'" (John 8:12). It was difficult—no, impossible—for those learned, esteemed leaders to see the light right in front of their eyes. It was easier for the woman who had been shamefully humbled to comprehend the Light.

It is often difficult for people who have made it on their own, especially those who have enjoyed a degree of success, to receive the gift of life, because humility is necessary for one to follow Christ. The world tells them to take pride in their accomplishments, yet this greatest attainment of all demands humility and reliance on One other than themselves. Jesus knew how difficult it was for the self-made and successful to resist pride and to humbly ask God to remake them in His image.

He told His disciples about a rich young man who had questioned Him about inheriting eternal life. "'I tell you the truth, it is hard for a rich man to enter the kingdom of heaven. Again I tell you, it is easier for a camel to go through the eye of a needle than for a rich man to enter the kingdom of God.' When the disciples heard this, they were greatly astonished and asked, 'Who then can be saved?' Jesus looked at them and said, 'With man this is impossible, but with God all things are possible'" (Matt. 19:23–26).

You may have heard the story of the small gate in the old wall of Jerusalem. After the main gates were shut at night, so the story goes, the only entrance was this small hole in the wall, called the Needle Gate. A camel, by getting down on its knees, could just barely squeeze through this hole in the wall. The camel, however, could not "go through the eye of the needle" without first unloading all the baggage on its back.

The first record of this story came from the writings of Saint Anselm in the eleventh century. In light of this story, Jesus' words about a camel attempting to pass through the eye of a needle makes greater sense. Unfortunately for those of us who need such explanations, there never was such a gate in the Jerusalem wall. When Jesus said the "eye of a needle," He apparently was saying exactly what He meant.[2]

Simply unloading our money and possessions, as the camel unloaded its baggage, does not squeeze us into the kingdom of God. Poverty doesn't earn a person eternal life, any more than prosperity does. When Jesus' disciples heard His explanation of these truths, they were astonished and asked Him, "'Who then can be saved?' Jesus looked at them and said, 'With man this is impossible, but with God all things are possible'" (vv. 25b–26). When we, too, ask this important question, we will discover that it is only by faith alone in what God can do for us—not in our works, not in our possessions, not in our titles—that we are saved.

88

Coming to Christ by our faith alone is the ultimate act of humility, for trusting in Christ's work *alone* means we first must lay aside any reliance we have on our own goodness or our own efforts. We can't trust in Christ alone while trusting in anything or anyone else. We must come, as did the corpse of Franz-Josef, "a humble sinner like us all," dead to self.

THE DISEASE

Naaman was the "Stormin' Norman" Schwarzkopf of his day. He was the commander of the armies of the king of Syria, a valiant warrior, a victor, and a national hero. He had gained great respect and financial reward for defeating the enemies of Syria. Ancient historian Josephus wrote that God had allowed the Syrian army to defeat wicked King Ahab of Israel because of the noble character of Naaman. (In fact, Josephus believed that the nameless archer who shot the arrow that killed Ahab was Naaman.)[3] Tragically, all his accomplishments became of little worth to him, as Naaman had become infected with leprosy.

The Bible gives a favorable description of Naaman and then abruptly says, in the original Hebrew, "a mighty man of valor—a leper." Leprosy was the most dreaded disease of that day. As some today might refer to Magic Johnson as "the outstanding basketball player of the Lakers—with AIDS," the people of Naaman's day would also label an individual with the feared disease of leprosy. The biblical description sounds awfully familiar.

Naaman faced a disease which had no known cure. The symptoms were painful and awful. There were basically two forms of leprosy, although both commonly appeared in the same patient, with the symptoms of one of the two usually predominant. One form caused sores to grow in the skin, in the mucous membranes of the nose, throat, and eyes, and sometimes in the internal organs. The sores, teeming with bacteria, could grow until they covered a person's entire body. They could be running sores with a horrible stench.

The second form of leprosy affected the nerves and caused a loss of sensation, especially in the extremities. The patient with this second form of leprosy faced various forms of paralysis and atrophy of tissues, with resultant loss of fingers, toes, and, sometimes, limbs. Death was inevitable for the person with leprosy; however, it could be a slow, agonizing death over the course of many years. A leper, like Naaman, fast became one of the living dead.

In the Old Testament, leprosy is a type or metaphor for sin. As leprosy cuts a person off from society, so sin alienates a person from God. Both leprosy's and sin's effects can spread until they consume a person's life. As leprosy can cause a person to lose sensation, sin causes sensitivity to God to be diminished. Like leprosy, sin produces "the living dead." Though a person is still alive outwardly, inwardly they are spiritually dead in their sin.

Paul wrote to the believers in Ephesus of their once being spiritually dead. "As for you, you were dead in your transgressions and sins, in which you used to live when you followed the ways of this world and of the ruler of the kingdom of the air, the spirit who is now at work in those who are disobedient. All of us also lived among them at one time, gratifying the cravings of our sinful nature and following its desires and thoughts" (Eph. 2:1–3a).

We all are born with the congenital disease of sin (see Rom. 3:23). We may not, however, be aware of its diagnosis, our prognosis, or the cure.

Naaman's leprosy was a horrible disease, separating him from his family and his command. His leprosy was having its impact on his body. He knew the diagnosis. It took no special revelation from God for Naaman to realize that he was dying of leprosy. He walked around with the realization of this disease day in and day out. He was not aware, however, that he was dying from a deadly sin disease.

Kevin began working for a large financial institution right out of college, in the late 1980s. His computer and management skills helped him move up the corporate ladder quickly. He purchased a beautiful condominium, a luxury sports car, and other symbols to reflect his success. He began experiencing a cash flow problem and soon needed roommates to help with expenses.

He knew his two new roommates' sexual preference before they moved into his condominium. He began experimenting with homosexual activity with his roommates. His sexual involvement grew. He began seeking new experiences with other gay partners. For two years his sexual activity increased. Upon contracting an STD, Kevin also received the diagnosis he was HIV-positive. The news of his health problems ran off his roommates.

Kevin was frightened and lonely. He knew he was ill but kept seeking sexual encounters. Though the disease did not prohibit his working at his career, he found no comfort in confiding in fellow employees, only increased isolation. He finally turned to family members for help. His family, on whom he thought he could count, shunned him because of his gay lifestyle.

Kevin grew depressed. He sought the help of a psychiatrist who offered only antidepressants and no answers to his problems. After multiple visits, he was no better off in his mental anguish and had developed a dependency on prescribed drugs to ease his pain. His was an emotional roller coaster, especially when the AIDS disease began to symptomatically manifest itself. No matter where he turned, there was no cure he could buy.

An episode of severe depression led to Kevin's consuming antidepressants and alcohol before driving to a business appointment one evening. With clouded judgment, Kevin failed to respond to the traffic challenges created by slick, rain-covered roads. Unable to stop suddenly at an intersection, he plowed into an oncoming truck and was killed instantly.

The life course Kevin chose failed to take him to the true Source of healing and love for his life. He failed to seek a personal relationship with Jesus Christ. For him, the pursuit of God's healing power seemed like a pointless venture. He lacked faith in this avenue that could have brought a cure for the sin-disease that was his greatest threat. He preferred the solutions offered by the world.

Sadly, this is how it is so often in our lives. We may recognize the need for healing of some disease or malady in our lives and miss all together our need for spiritual healing.

"What is your greatest discovery, Sir James?" asked an interviewer of the discoverer of chloroform.

"That I am a sinner," answered the saintly man, "and that Jesus Christ is my Savior."[4]

This was, by far, his greatest discovery!

It took Commander Naaman some time to make that discovery. He sought only a cure for his leprosy. What he found to be promising was a reported cure. A servant girl who had been taken captive from Israel told her mistress, Naaman's wife, of a prophet in Samaria who could heal Naaman's disease. Apparently Naaman's body was not so decayed by leprosy that he was unable to pursue a cure. Desperately seeking the one cure he desired, Naaman traveled to Samaria in Israel.

THE ROAD TO A CURE

One of the fascinating aspects of travel is the unpredictableness of what may occur to the traveler while on the journey. I find this to be true in taking business trips. If traveling by plane, there can be delays, lost luggage, or crying babies. There can also be serendipitous upgrades, relaxation, or fascinating seatmates. On a recent flight, I had expected to do a little reading and some study. Instead, I found myself engaged in a fascinating conversation with my seatmate.

He was a successful entrepreneur. His business ventures had netted him millions of dollars. A new golf invention he and his son developed earned them $1.5 million in the last year alone. His life, however, was not without difficulties. He was dealing with the issue of guilt because he did not want to visit an older brother—an alcoholic—who lay dying of cancer in the hospital. It seems his brother had abused him physically as a boy and verbally as a man. His brother was not a Christian.

My seatmate had a knowledge of Christ. I shared with him a tract which explained the way to Christ. I encouraged him to read it, prayerfully consider its message, and then share it with his brother. I don't know what transpired between this man and his brother or this man and His God. I do know, however, the flight together was a divine appointment.

We never know what awaits us as we travel. God often lets us come into contact with those who need our help in pointing the way to Him. Such was the case an earlier time in my life, during the Vietnam War. I took a bus to a speaking engagement in another city. Behind me, on the bus, was seated a young soldier. When we were en route, I moved back and struck up a conversation with this young man. Of particular interest to me was his being from Knoxville. We talked about our native state, Tennessee, and also about his impending departure to Vietnam. He was anxious about what lay ahead in that distant land, but he was ready to serve his country. The conversation soon turned to matters of the faith. I asked him about his spiritual readiness to face the battles of life.

He was not a Christian, but he was, at that moment, receptive to the things of God. During that divine appointment on the bus, he embraced Jesus Christ as his Lord and Savior. Now, he expressed hope for what was ahead in his tour in Vietnam. I was excited about what God had accomplished on that bus trip.

Sometime later, while visiting a hospital in Nashville, I picked up the day's issue of *The Nashville Tennessean*. As was customary at that time, the newspaper ran a listing of those wounded or killed in battle. I quickly glanced at the list to see if there were any men from our city on it. There was a soldier from Knoxville listed as killed in battle. It was the young man I had met on the bus. His journey on the bus had prepared him, more than he had ever expected, for what faced him in life's journey.

Naaman departed on what he hoped would be the road to a cure. He took with him ten talents of silver, six thousand shekels of gold, and ten sets of clothing—valued around $1.5 million at today's rate of exchange—all to buy a cure. He eventually found his way to the door of the prophet Elisha's house.

> So Naaman went with his horses and chariots and stopped at the door of Elisha's house. Elisha sent a messenger to say to him, "Go and wash yourself seven times in the Jordan, and your flesh will be restored and you will be cleansed." But Naaman went away angry and said, "I thought that he would surely come out to me and stand and call on the name of the LORD his God, wave his hand over the spot and cure me of my leprosy. Are not Abana and Pharpar, the rivers of Damascus, better than any of the waters of Israel? Couldn't I wash in them and be cleansed?" So he turned and went off in a rage. (2 Kings 5:9–12)

Elisha was not impressed by Naaman's entourage of chariots, soldiers, horses, and servants. He didn't even pay this great warrior and commander the courtesy of coming out to greet him or offer to receive him as a respected guest in his home. There was no pomp or ceremony to which Naaman was accustomed. Elisha only sent a messenger instructing Naaman to go and take a bath in that muddy little river. How disgraceful and undignified!

Naaman wanted to be healed on his own terms and in a way more appropriate for a man of his station. He felt he had already humbled himself enough just coming there. His money and his position should grant him whatever concession necessary to get around normal healing procedures. When Naaman's pretentious agenda did not mesh with God's requirements of humility, he left—enraged. Naaman is like many who go the distance of their journey, to the very doorway of eternal life, and then get offended at the gospel and walk away.

What is there about the gospel that can be such an offense? It is a matter of accepting the fact that salvation is by faith and "not by works, so that no one can boast" (Eph. 2:9). It's hard for a person of affluence to believe money doesn't buy everything. It is equally hard for a person of high position to believe having the right name doesn't open every door. It may be even harder for someone who considers himself or herself a "good person" to confess he or she

93

has no inherent goodness meriting salvation. All are bankrupt and have *nothing* to offer. One can only approach the Father in humility—empty-handed—by faith to accept the salvation He has accomplished.

Naaman's road to recovery was detoured by his own pride. He probably would have taken the road back to Damascus, died a horrible death, and we never would have heard of him; except some of his servants took the risk to approach their superior, Naaman, about the correct course that should be taken. "'My father, if the prophet had told you to do some great thing, would you not have done it? How much more, then, when he tells you, "Wash, and be cleansed"!' So he went down and dipped himself in the Jordan seven times, as the man of God had told him, and his flesh was restored and became clean like that of a young boy" (2 Kings 5:13–14).

Naaman must have been an odd sight—a man whose body and skin were so eaten away it probably would sicken one to look at him, dressed in the most lavish of robes, standing there in his ornate chariot. Something in what was said to him by his servants made Naaman stop his retreat and realize he had been off-course in seeking a cure. He could not save himself.

Putting aside all the medals, the clothing, and everything which signified importance and respect, the humbled sinner, Naaman, went down to the Jordan. He stepped in the muddy waters and washed himself as he was instructed to do—not once, but seven times!

When the seventh bathing was complete, an amazing miracle took place. Not only was the progress of the disease halted, but Naaman's body was restored to its pre-disease state (see v. 14). It was obvious to all—including Naaman—that the cure had come from God alone. No person had bought the cure. No person had dictated the terms of the cure. The God of Israel alone was responsible for the miracle that had taken place.

At that point on his journey, Naaman experienced more than he had ever anticipated. For in that moment of realization of who was in charge of the physical realm, Naaman realized the God of Israel was the one true God of all realms—physical and spiritual. His healing was now complete.

We, like Naaman, must be stripped of our pride to receive the healing God has for us in our lives. If we will take the plunge and accept by humble faith the course God has chosen to save us— that is, the road to Calvary—then we, too, can be restored. Jesus died for our sins, offering Himself as a sacrifice that He might cleanse us with His blood and make us new. It is through His merit alone that we can be perfectly cleansed. The lines of an old hymn remind me of Naaman.

> There is a fountain filled with blood
> Drawn from Emmanuel's veins;
> And sinners, plunged beneath that flood,
> Lose all their guilty stains.[5]

Naaman's story could have had a much different—and tragic—ending should Naaman have chosen to return home without visiting the Jordan River. I am sure, at the outset of his journey, he had no idea where his original course was taking him or where future turns would take him.

Our perspective has everything to do with our evaluation of where we are headed in life's course. There is no greater instance in which a poor perspective can detour us than in the perspective of our relationship to God. This can most definitely send us down the wrong pathway, away from healing and abundant life. If a person perceives that the sin gap between God and man is immeasurably wide, then he will be more aware of his desperate need for the atoning sacrifice of Jesus Christ. If, on the other hand, a person perceives the moral gap between God and man as rather narrow, then he may feel that he can bridge the gap merely by his own efforts or good deeds.

Earning salvation by one's own effort, one's own sacrifice, and the quality of one's own character is foundational to the teaching of all religions except Christianity, for it appeals to human nature. If one, like Naaman, perceives there is no moral separation at all, then he will be hostile to the suggestion he needs a Savior. A person cannot realize he needs to "be saved" until he first realizes he has a desperate need of a cure for his sin-diseased state and he is helpless to save himself. Then, only by following God's directions, can he be restored and made whole.

God is a God of perfect justice; however, He chooses to give mercy to those of us who humbly and repentantly approach Him, rather than giving the justice we deserve. It is amazing that He would rather forgive us on the basis of what Christ has done than judge us on the basis of what we have done. The most liberating experience of life is when we realize, though we are fatally sin-diseased and lost on the road to a cure, we can be completely cleansed and saved—by faith alone in Jesus Christ.

95

THE COST OF HEALING

Medical costs are staggering. Any of us who have visited a physician, had a prescription filled, or stayed in a hospital recently know well how expensive medical costs are in our country today. If we don't have insurance coverage, then we'd better stay healthy.

After Naaman received such excellent medical care, he was ready to foot the bill. Out of gratitude for what God had done, he returned to the home of Elisha. "He stood before him and said, 'Now I know that there is no God in all the world except in Israel. Please accept now a gift from your servant'" (v. 15). Remember, the payment he expected to render amounted approximately to $1.5 million! That's a pretty good fee for even the best doctors today!

There was more for Naaman to learn. His money was not what God wanted in response to what He had done for him—for this might lead him or others to believe that God's healing could be bought. Again, Naaman did not have a clear perception of what was expected of him. His cleansing was so effective he desired to do something for the Lord. His desire to respond was good.

Salvation does demand a response. Martin Luther declared that "Justification (salvation) is by faith alone, but not by a faith that is alone." God does not wait on our good works to declare us justified. Our good works, however, should soon serve as evidence of the radical change that has occurred in our lives. James said that "faith without deeds [works] is dead" (James 2:26). Works will attest to the truth of our salvation.

Once dying in sin, Naaman now possessed a living faith. His faith immediately produced evidence of his total cleansing. His desire was to worship the God of Israel. He assumed that Jehovah God could only be worshiped on the sacred soil of Israel. He asked Elisha, "'Please let me, your servant, be given as much earth as a pair of mules can carry, for your servant will never again make burnt offerings and sacrifices to any other god but the LORD'" (v. 17). Naaman wanted to change his worship—from false gods— to the one, true God. He apparently planned to erect an altar to Jehovah God in Syria.

Naaman was also convicted of a wrongful practice in his life and desired forgiveness for his sin. One of his duties to the king of Syria was to accompany the king to the temple of Rimmon, a false deity. At the temple, the king would take Naaman's arm and lean on him as he bowed to worship Rimmon. This forced Naaman to bow, also, to support the king's weight. Naaman did this as a part of his duties, no longer out of worship of this lesser god. Unlike Daniel, he did not yet possess the matured and strong faith to refuse to enter the temple and compromise his faith. He asked Elisha for forgiveness ahead of time!

Elisha, understanding Naaman's young faith and the potential good that might be accomplished as the king's commander, instructed him to "go in peace" (v. 19). Peace. That certainly was a new concept for troubled Naaman. To be able to live a life of peace—without the curse of leprosy and the burden of unforgiven sin—would be a blessing beyond anything this warrior had ever imagined possible. His journey had led him to a cure and to a faith which made him whole.

THE EPIDEMIC OF CHEAP GRACE

Many people claim to be saved, but there is no substantiating evidence of their faith, only hearsay of what Christ has done in their lives. Their empty words lack credibility. No good works proceed from their professed faith. This is sometimes referred to as "cheap grace," grace without the evidence of the transforming Son of God and without discipleship to the Lord of lords.

Dietrich Bonhoeffer, later hanged by the Nazis in 1945 for his faith, called cheap grace "the deadly enemy of our church."[6] Professing Christians who yield only lip service to the Master are detrimental to the credibility of true believers whose lives bear the fruit of their faith. The world often wrongly perceives the Christian faith on the basis of the cheap grace which is much too abundant. The fellowship and work of the church are hurt by these superficial Christians.

Gehazi, Elisha's servant, was a professing believer in Jehovah God. His cheap grace, as evidenced by his actions in the remainder of this story, stand in stark contrast to the true faith of Naaman. He hurriedly followed Naaman on the road to Syria and approached the restored convert. Gehazi duped him into believing that Elisha had changed his mind about accepting money from Naaman. He said the funds and clothing were needed to support two young itinerant prophets. Naaman gave him quite a substantial amount. When Gehazi returned, he hid these in his house. He then deceitfully faced Elisha. He lied about having been away.

This is how the false practices of too many professing Christians occur. They continue to live as they did when they were dead in sin—lying, stealing, compromising their integrity and their faith.

97

No good works, only selfish indulgences, are evident. There is an epidemic of Gehazis. While their diseased symptoms may be masked, their infection is contagious to a dying world. The spread of their fatal disease will be halted one day. The cure for them on that day will be condemning judgment, not saving grace.

Gehazi faced the judgment of God. Elisha pronounced the divine retribution on him: "Naaman's leprosy will cling to you and to your descendants forever" (v. 27). His payment for professing a false faith and for pursuing a course of sinful deeds was great. His pathway led to his incurring God's wrath through the dreaded disease of the living dead.

Where is your course taking you? What is your perspective of your relationship to God and your inclination to sin? Have you realized the vastness of the sin gap in your life and sought a bridge to God through Jesus Christ? Have you been restored to wholeness through salvation, instead of wasting away in a sin-diseased state? In salvation through God's Son there is hope, there is healing; and there is strength to travel life's way. "Therefore, since we have been justified through faith, we have peace with God through our Lord Jesus Christ, through whom we have gained access by faith into this grace in which we now stand. And we rejoice in the hope of the glory of God. Not only so, but we also rejoice in our sufferings, because we know that suffering produces perseverance; perseverance, character; and character, hope. And hope does not disappoint us, because God has poured out his love" (Rom. 5:1a).

CHAPTER SEVEN

OUR PERSPECTIVE OF INTEGRITY

After reading some of the surveys from the book *The Day America Told the Truth*, I am further convinced that there is, indeed, an integrity crisis in the United States. The book's extensive research reveals some startling facts about our culture of the nineties. When Americans were asked the question, "What would you do for ten million dollars," responses indicated

- 25 percent would abandon their families,

- 25 percent would abandon their churches,

- 23 percent would become a prostitute for a week,

- 3 percent would put their children up for adoption, and

- 7 percent of Americans would kill a stranger.[1]

This integrity crisis permeates all age groups. The Hosephson Institute of Ethics in Los Angeles found 33 percent of high-school students had shoplifted in the previous twelve months and 61 percent had cheated on an exam.[2]

Perhaps the most shocking of all research for Christians reveals that *there is little statistical difference between the ethical practices of the religious and the nonreligious.*[3] Forty-three percent of non-church attendees admitted to stealing work supplies, compared to 37 percent of church attendees. Seventeen percent of those who did not go to church responded that they used the company

99

phone for long-distance personal calls, as compared to 13 percent of church-going respondents.

THE MOST VALUED OF ALL POSSESSIONS

Our church is blessed to have as one of its vital ministries an outstanding school for students, K–12. The mission statement of the school should be a battle cry for all who teach young people everywhere. Especially appropriate is the section which deals with this issue of integrity: Preparing children for life . . . who choose character before career. Our school takes seriously the task of instructing our students in matters of ethical conduct, moral behavior, and virtuous living. The challenge in instructing today's youth is in helping them to see *why* something is right or wrong according to God's perfect standard and, then, instilling in them the desire to choose the more excellent standard. Our church's mission through our school is to produce excellently trained and equipped Christian adults who put God first in all decisions.[4]

Choosing what is right or what is wrong is a dilemma we have always faced. I still remember a boyhood incident when I dealt with this issue of integrity. My friends and I had finished ball practice. We left school and headed to the fountain of the local drugstore. We were famished. All were buying sodas and snacks when I remembered I didn't have any money to buy anything. Glancing this way and that way, as I kept an eye open for Doc (the pharmacist and owner), I stole a Butterfinger candy bar. I sat next to the other guys and ate it as quickly as possible, so Doc would not catch me. I have never eaten anything as hard to swallow as that candy bar! I just knew that at any second Doc was going to call the police and have me hauled away to jail. I left that drug store as quickly as I could, with my heart pounding so loudly that I knew others could hear it.

I did not sleep a wink that night. I tossed and I turned. God the Holy Spirit was causing my young conscience to be bothered in one of those maturing ways. I knew what I must do. I prayed God would forgive me—and the police would not come to my house and arrest me. The next day, I gathered up the change to make restitution for my crime. I went to the drugstore and called Doc over to talk with me. I confessed to stealing the candy bar, of which he said he was not aware. I asked him to accept my payment, but he refused.

He put his hands on my shoulder and told me that what I had done was very wrong, he wanted me to keep my money, and he expected for me to never do anything like it again. Doc was a special man with a true understanding of the torment I had just experienced. Butterfingers, to this day, serve as a reminder to me of the value of integrity.

The word *integrity* is derived from a Latin word which literally means wholeness, soundness, or togetherness. It refers to the integration or the "togetherness" of all parts. When a woman gives into sexual temptations and engages in premarital sex, she is said to have *lost* her virginity. The same is true for a man. What they lost is not something physical, but rather, they lost their wholeness. What they once possessed *dis-integrates;* that is, the integrity is no longer there.

Solomon wrote, "Above all else, guard your heart, for it is the wellspring of life" (Prov. 4:23). Your character and integrity are your most valuable possessions. You do not have to be rich to obtain these, but they may cost you everything to keep.

Noah Webster once said, "Conscience is the most sacred of all property." There are scores of books published yearly, this being one more, endeavoring to point out the secrets, the keys, to personal peace and happiness. Yet, very few ever get around to the idea that our greatest possession—our greatest source of peace, satisfaction, and self-esteem—is our own integrity. (Of course, our salvation is necessary for us to have this wholeness.) Virtue, honor, and a clear conscience are the best things we can possess—so much so, that they are worth the loss of all other things to hold on tightly to them.

Nevertheless, people commonly forfeit their integrity, thinking what they will gain in the exchange will bring them greater happiness. Soon they come to the gut-wrenching realization that they have, as a result, become more miserable than they ever imagined possible. They have lost something of immense value which is difficult, if not impossible, to regain.

TRAITS OF INTEGRITY

Up until about fifty years ago, character was considered the essential ingredient for living a good and successful life. The most important things to have were honesty, industry, and fairness—the Golden Rule kind of stuff. In the last twenty years, I have definitely noticed a mind shift. Today, success and happiness are considered by most to be the result of "people skills"—positive attitudes, management techniques, communications skills, and public relations.

The average nineties-kind-of-businessperson understands, from a public relations standpoint, it is important to *appear* to have integrity. That does not mean most believe *actual* personal integrity is integral in making one successful in life. Daily, the newscasts and newspapers are filled with the debate over issues of integrity. There is apparent division in our country over what truly matters in the area of integrity.

What are the marks of those who choose to live their lives with integrity? Here are three traits I believe can change lives.

INTEGRITY TRAIT 1: THE MARK OF TRUTHFULNESS

Lying has become such an accepted practice many people do it without even thinking about its being wrong. In their survey, Patterson and Kim found that 91 percent of Americans said that they lied regularly. Eighty-six percent said they lied regularly to their parents, and 75 percent reported they lied regularly to their friends.[5] There are three basic reasons that people lie.

First of all, *they lie to cover up.* Who knows what really happened on the evening of June 12, 1994, at 857 South Bundy Drive? Where was O. J.? Who really killed Nicole Brown and Ronald Goldman? O. J. Simpson was found innocent by the jury, but, in reality, the trial is not over. Mr. Simpson will stand trial at least one more time—when he, like all the rest of us, stands before the King of kings and the Judge of judges.

People go to all extremes to cover up the facts, to discredit the evidence, and to shift the blame. Yet a character trait of a man or woman of integrity is that they tell the whole truth and nothing but the truth. They are straightforward, refusing to shade the facts or bend the truth. They consistently tell it like it is—just as it will be done before God, our Judge.

Second, *people lie to get along.* They don't want to make waves, cause trouble, or alienate people. To be a person of integrity does not mean that one has to be tactless or ugly, only truthful in love. Many people's desire to avoid uncomfortable situations causes them to stumble. In their attempt to be peacemakers at all costs, they become liars.

Third, *people lie to get ahead.* Lying to make a sale, cheating to pass a test, or falsifying documents are, to many, just the normal, accepted ways of doing what it takes to get ahead. "Everyone else

102

is doing it, so why shouldn't I?" We hear this often said. What we fail to hear is the cost of losing one's wholeness as a result of these choices.

INTEGRITY TRAIT 2: THE MARK OF HONESTY

In a paper presented at a symposium on employee theft sponsored by the American Psychological Association, the speaker pointed out that $8 billion are lost every year from the inventory of our stores and shops: 10 percent by clerical error, 30 percent by shoplifting, and 60 percent, (or $16 million daily) by employee theft.[6]

How do we stay honest in a corrupt world? Choose Christ's standard, not the world's. We cannot be on the lookout for ways to beat the system. We are not owed anything worth compromising our integrity to attain it. Some simple practices of honesty need to become habits. Don't use the company phone to place personal long-distance calls. Don't exaggerate the expense or mileage accounts. Don't take office equipment home or use it without permission. Don't fudge on your income tax return, regardless of what you think about the budgetary policies of the federal government.

Your conscience will get you. One man wrote a letter to the IRS: "I lied on my tax return and have a guilty conscience. Enclosed is a check for $100. If that doesn't clear up my conscience, I'll send you the rest."[7]

Some matters of honesty may seem insignificant initially. If left unchecked, however, the compromising of one's honesty will cause a deterioration of one's character, which, needless to say, deteriorates one's relationship with God. Eventually, restraint may become so weakened, one finds it easy to cheat anyone and to steal bigger things. Sooner or later, it will catch up with the one who is not honest.

I know a man who was a bank teller in a small town for over thirty years. Eventually, he became the head teller. He tells fascinating stories of tellers—who were respected citizens and church members—embezzling money from the bank. There seemed to be a pattern with these people. At first they would only borrow a small amount out of their cash drawers. Once they started, however, it was hard to stop. Before long, they would be out thousands of dollars from their cash drawers. For a while, they could somehow falsify their balances and get away with it. Then the inevitable would happen. They would go on vacation and the head teller would decide to reconcile their drawers. They always got caught, and, by law, the FBI had to be called in to arrest them. You can bet on it; your sins will find you out.

INTEGRITY TRAIT 3: THE MARK OF TRUSTWORTHINESS

Keeping our word should be one of the distinguishing marks of our Christian lifestyle. We should be people who do absolutely what we say we are going to do. Seems like a simple thing, doesn't it? It's amazing how many people don't do it.

A woman in our church who works with the preschoolers came to me one day and said, "I can't be involved in this ministry any longer. I'm a single parent, supporting three children by myself. Even though I have plenty of excuses, I try to make sure I never shirk my parental duties. I have a problem with some of the parents who volunteered for extended care and think nothing of calling me at the last minute to pass their duty on to me. They simply say, 'We have decided to go out of town, so we won't be there.' Even when I remind them that if they don't get a substitute, we may have to close the room, they don't seem to care. There are others with whom I have bent over backward to cooperate, and, still, they simply don't show up. I'm tired of all the feeble excuses. Why can't these people do what they said they would do? I can't cover for them any longer."

I was likewise troubled when I heard someone say, "I don't like doing business with Christians." What was even more troubling to me was this was not the first time I had heard such a comment. When I thought about what could be at the root of this, I realized sometimes people overstate their problems. While some people just have an animosity toward Christians in general, others may have had valid reasons based on their previous business dealings with Christians.

This is a tragic situation because Christians should go the extra mile to display integrity and honesty with nonbelievers. When we as Christians do less than an adequate job or fail to render a promised service, the impact is magnified because unbelievers expect more of Christians. They know enough about Christ and the Bible to hold us to a higher standard than they do others.

We need to make commitments because they sharpen our lives. What we commit to do sometimes is the impetus to our doing greater things for the Lord and His service. Society needs people on whom they can count. We must remember not to carelessly squander our integrity by not keeping our word.

FIVE LESSONS FROM BABYLON

The world is filled with people today who look like they have it all together on the outside; but on the inside, they are falling apart. There is an emptiness and deadness inside because they have lost their wholeness, their integrity. Somewhere along the way, they sold their souls to gain happiness or success in life.

In the story, "The Devil and Daniel Webster," Daniel sells his soul to the devil in return for material prosperity. There is another Daniel, not a fictitious character, but a real individual about whom we read in the Old Testament. This Daniel was willing to forsake all to keep his integrity. He is the Daniel to whom the Bible refers three times as "the beloved of the LORD" (see Dan. 9:23; 10:11, 17, KJV).

Daniel lived at the time when the Babylonians conquered the Egyptians at the battle of Carchemish (605 B.C.). After the defeat of the Egyptians, Babylon was the super power that dominated all of the Middle East. Nebuchadnezzar had already defeated Israel and dispersed its ten tribes to other nations. He then turned his attention to the southern kingdom of Judah.

The Babylonians came south to the city of Jerusalem. The city was eventually destroyed. Those who were not killed were taken captive and exiled to Babylon. Nebuchadnezzar was not content simply to have the leading cities of these conquered nations under his control. He wanted their finest young men taken to Babylon to be trained as his government personnel. Among those chosen from Jerusalem were Daniel and the three men who would become his closest friends. They were probably teenagers at the time.

These Hebrew youths were most likely between the ages of thirteen and fifteen. They were "young men without any physical defect, handsome, showing aptitude for every kind of learning, well informed, quick to understand, and qualified to serve in the king's palace" (Dan. 1:4). These teenagers were amazing in more ways than these, for they had already learned how to keep their integrity in very difficult and trying situations. By their example we have been provided lessons about maintaining integrity in a hostile world.

105

LESSON 1: BE CERTAIN OF WHAT IS RIGHT

Daniel and friends were brought to Babylon to be trained for three years, after which they would serve in the court of King Nebuchadnezzar. Their educational program included instruction in "the language and literature of the Babylonians" (Dan. 1:4c). Their curriculum probably consisted of studies in Babylonian philosophy, religion, astrology, science, medicine, and even magic. Along with their training, they were given a daily ration of the king's choicest food and best wine. This ration provided the first challenge. "But Daniel resolved not to defile himself with the royal food and wine, and he asked the chief official for permission not to defile himself this way" (Dan. 1:8).

Whether it was food forbidden by the Old Testament law or it was the fact that it had first been ceremonially sacrificed to idols, to eat it was to violate his integrity. More than food or Daniel's integrity was at stake here. To refuse the king's choicest food and wine would be an insult, especially coming from a slave. People who insulted Babylonian kings usually didn't live long. I can almost hear the voices of the Jewish comrades of Daniel and his three friends: "Look, Dan, the Lord has miraculously spared our lives, and we've got it pretty good compared to what happened to other guys we know. Since He brought us here, surely God wouldn't mind our having a little Babylonian food. Besides, if you don't back off, you're going to ruin things for all the rest of us!"

Isn't it amazing how people can rationalize things in their minds and come up with ethical conclusions which are 180 degrees in the wrong direction? In their doing wrong, they convince themselves they are doing right. They, in effect, deceive their own hearts to justify their own desires. They are liars in that they lie to themselves and think they have fooled God in the process. A great challenge to one's integrity is the ability to honestly evaluate a situation and to discern what is right.

The Babylonian program is a classic example of brain-washing. Sinclair Ferguson points out four ways in which the Babylonians did so.[8] First, the youths were *isolated* from their families, their homes, their history, their cultural traditions, and their religious practices. Second, they were *indoctrinated.* The chief official's goal in providing the educational program (earlier delineated) was to convert the monotheistic Hebrews to Babylonian polytheism. Third, they *compromised* their integrity by forcing them to violate and forsake the commands of their religion. King Nebuchadnezzar wanted these young people to serve the false gods of Babylon and adopt that nation's heathen lifestyle. Fourth, *they changed their identity.* They were given new Babylonian names (see Dan. 1:7). The reasoning behind doing so was to completely change their identities and to make them into Babylonians.

What Nebuchadnezzar did, Satan seeks to do to each of us today: to isolate us from the things of God, to indoctrinate us with a "new truth," to compromise our integrity, and, finally, to get us to forget who we really are as children of God.

Viktor Frankl, an Austrian psychologist who survived the death camps of Nazi Germany, found within himself the ability to rise above the humiliating and dehumanizing circumstances and to become an observer of what was taking place. He was intrigued by what made it possible for some people to survive. Afterward he wrote of what he saw:

> We who lived in concentration camps can remember the men who walked through the huts comforting others, giving away their last piece of bread. They may have been few in number, but they offer sufficient proof that everything can be taken from a man but one thing: the last of human freedoms—to choose one's attitude in any given set of circumstances, to choose one's own way.
>
> And there were always choices to make. Every day, every hour, offered the opportunity to make a decision which determined whether you would or would not submit to those powers which threatened to rob you of your very self, your inner freedom; which determined whether or not you would become the plaything of the circumstance.[9]

The design of the Babylonian training was to reprogram and to control the very souls of these Hebrew teenagers. Perhaps there were many who became Babylonians, inside and out. For Daniel and his friends, they possessed that which they would not let go—their integrity and their identity.

LESSON 2: STAND FOR WHAT IS RIGHT

Shadrach, Meshach, and Abednego had the same spirit as Daniel. They were smart, diligent men, and, at Daniel's request, Nebuchadnezzar had appointed them as administrators over the province of Babylon.

Every one of us will be tested at points of integrity. Though our integrity may go unchallenged for a time, the day will surely come

107

when we must make a stand for what is right—or fall by what is wrong. The challenge came for Daniel's friends when Nebuchadnezzar set up a statue and commanded everyone to bow down to worship. Shadrach, Meshach, and Abednego refused to compromise their integrity by compromising their devotion to God.

The refusal of these three Hebrew transplants wound up getting them thrown into the fiery furnace. Notice their attitude: "Shadrach, Meshach and Abednego replied to the king, 'O Nebuchadnezzar, we do not need to defend ourselves before you in this matter. If we are thrown into the blazing furnace, the God we serve is able to save us from it, and he will rescue us from your hand, O king. But even if he does not, we want you to know, O king, that we will not serve your gods or worship the image of gold you have set up'" (Dan. 3:16–18).

Nebuchadnezzar was enraged. The Scriptures say, "his attitude toward them changed" (Dan. 3:19). He then ordered Shadrach, Meshach, and Abednego bound and the furnace heated seven times hotter than normal. I'm not sure what good that was supposed to do. If they were going to be thrown into the furnace, seven times hotter would only get it over faster. Actually, what so enraged the king was, even though he possessed absolute dominion over everything in the kingdom—even the souls of his subjects—he was unable to take from these three men something they possessed. They were like those prisoners Viktor Frankl observed—free on the inside even though they were sentenced to death.

A somewhat common practice in the business world is to consider people who take a stand for issues of conscience as suspect, threatening, or even perhaps as losers who should be passed over by others who are more willing to play the game. This should not discourage the Christan businessperson. I truly believe that taking a stand for issues of character, honesty, and fair practice will, in the long run, cause one to prosper in all the right ways. However, if one is going to be a man or woman of integrity, one needs to realize that it may, in the short run, be very costly.

Jon, a young executive in our congregation, recently got a big promotion. Part of his job responsibilities includes entertaining other executives who come into town on business. One of the things the traveling businessmen enjoy doing while in Orlando is going to a men's club, the type where the focus is on scantily clad young women. Jon refuses to go with them, and in doing so, runs the risk of losing his job.

Jon's refusal to compromise his integrity for his job has drawn comments from fellow executives and managers. Encouraging comments came from some out-of-state managers. They thanked him for having the convictions to make such a stand. They went on to say how they admired him as a gentleman and as a Christian. Jon's stand is precisely the type of stand that validates a Christian witness.

Is there any real difference between people who, on the one hand, act with integrity as long as it benefits them and people who, on the other hand, always acquire what they want by cheating and stealing? They both have a morality of convenience and are willing to forsake conscience (that is, God) to get what they think they want or that which they think is due them.

I have known people who have gone through difficult situations and are bitter at God for not rescuing them from their own fiery furnaces. They feel as though the Lord abandoned them; so, what difference does faithfulness to Him make now? They feel justified in their moral lapses because God didn't come through for them as they thought He should.

These three young friends of Daniel's were committed to do what was right without respect to the outcome—whether it benefited them or cost them everything. They so greatly valued their integrity, they were willing to pay the ultimate price to stand for what was right.

LESSON 3: SPEAK ONLY WHAT IS RIGHT

Daniel advanced in the service of the king. In fact, he was so highly regarded for his integrity and his wisdom, he served as an advisor to two Babylonian kings and to Cyrus (the Medo-Persian king who conquered the Babylonians) as well. With each new "boss," Daniel's willingness to speak the truth was challenged.

Nebuchadnezzar had a vivid dream which greatly disturbed him. There was a great tree which grew until its height reached the sky and was visible to the ends of the earth. It provided shade and food for all creatures. Nebuchadnezzar saw in his dream an angelic observer command the tree to be chopped down and cut into pieces, leaving only a stump. The angel went on to address an individual saying that he would be given the mind of a beast and he would be drenched with the dew of heaven for seven periods of time.

None of the magicians or diviners were able to explain the dream to Nebuchadnezzar. That was strange because the interpretation of the dream appears to be rather obvious. Nebuchadnezzar (who else?) was the great tree, and the angel was prophesying his being cut down to size. Perhaps, it was not that they were all so dense in understanding; of course, they knew what the dream meant. It was simply that no one was willing or brave enough to say that which was so obvious.

I can picture it. The wise men are sitting around arguing about who is going to be the one to go in and tell Nebuchadnezzar that he is about to be turned into an idiot and live in the fields like a wild animal? Each guy has a good reason for not telling the king. Maybe they should attempt to explain the dream in a way that being cut down to a stump means something beneficial to the king! In any case, no one volunteers to speak the truth.

One of Hans Christian Anderson's most enduring stories[10] is a tale of subjects who were fearful to speak the truth. It is the story of an emperor, so fond of new clothes, he spent all of his money on them. He had little concern for royal matters.

One day two rascals came to town pretending to be weavers and said they could weave the most exquisite material imaginable. Not only was this material beautiful, but it would become invisible to any person who was unfit for his office or was exceptionally stupid. The emperor gave the would-be weavers a large sum of money to make clothing for him from this material. Not only would he have a new wardrobe, but also an ingenious way of distinguishing wise men from fools.

As time went on, the emperor sent some of his ministers to check on the progress of the weavers. Unwilling to be discredited as a fool, each minister praised their work as the most beautiful fabric they had ever seen. Finally, the day came for the royal parade. The new clothes were presented to the emperor. He, too, not wanting to admit his own unworthiness, praised the weavers.

Word had spread throughout the kingdom about the king's marvelous new clothes and everyone was waiting with great expectations to see them. The masses cheered the emperor and shouted compliments about his beautiful new clothes as he processed by them. It was a lone, small boy who innocently spoke up and rather loudly said to his father what had been obvious all along. Others overheard him, and soon his bold words were echoed by many others:

"The emperor has no clothes!"

It is amazing what fear and greed will do to a person's discernment. If one squints and strains hard enough, one may actually begin to see clothes on the emperor. This seems to be the case with the Babylonian wise men. They were squinting and straining to see an interpretation which was not there. Possibly they were so blinded by their fear and desire to advance in the eyes of the king that they couldn't see anything at all.

Whatever the case, Daniel was like the little boy who spoke that which was obvious. He simply and boldly spoke the truth as he saw it. This was not an isolated incident in speaking the truth. It was, for him, one of many consistent choices as a believer.

Years later Nebuchadnezzar died, and his son, Belshazzar, became king. At a feast given for a thousand guests, the arrogant and drunken Belshazzar ordered the vessels, taken by his father from the temple in Jerusalem, be used to serve wine to his nobles. God's judgment was proclaimed by a hand that appeared and wrote on the wall: "Mene, Mene, Tekel, Parsin" (Dan. 5:25).

After none of the wise men could interpret the writing, Daniel was summoned. Daniel refused to take money for his services and proclaimed the meaning to the king. "God has numbered the days of your reign and brought it to an end. . . . You have been weighed on the scales and found wanting.   Your kingdom is divided and given to the Medes and Persians (Dan. 5:26b–28).

Daniel was not a man-pleaser. He refused to allow his integrity to be compromised. He could not be intimidated or bought. In the same respect, he was a faithful and loyal servant to each king he served. Whether he was rewarded, promoted, or thrown into a lions' den, Daniel spoke what was true. For these reasons, he was permitted to speak for God.

LESSON 4: DO ALWAYS WHAT IS RIGHT

We're six hundred miles from home. Who's gonna know? Those had to be the thoughts of the Hebrew teenagers as they gobbled down the king's meat. Who would know or even care if they did as the Babylonians while in Babylon? Teenagers, from the time of Cain and Abel to the present day, have had to come to terms with their own integrity. What will they do when no one is looking?

A few years ago the *Orlando Sentinel* ran a story of a young tennis player in a championship match. What caught my attention was this young lady's handling of a bad call. She was aware that an opponent's shot was in bounds when the linesman called the

111

shot out of bounds. It was a critical point in the match; however, she knew she had been the beneficiary of a bad call. She approached the umpire's chair and told him that the ball was clearly on the line. The call was changed, and her opponent went on to narrowly win the game, set, and match. The girl didn't hesitate to set things straight, whether or not it meant the match. She said it was "just the right thing to do."

Adults face this same thing. Last night I was watching an exciting NBA game. As the clock counted down the final minute, the lead was exchanged a half dozen times. The losing team gained possession of the ball with less than five seconds left in the game. The point guard drove the ball to the basket and was hacked on the arm in the process. The foul was not called. The player did not score. The game was over. Although my favorite team won, I was forced to think about this "big win." The announcers commented on the foul. The video replays clearly showed the foul. The point guard, more than likely, knew he fouled the other guy, but he said nothing. No one expected him to. The sports analysts concluded that the fouls had been "evened out." The player, therefore, was "justified" in his silence.

In marriage, when we are attracted to someone other than our spouse, how do we handle temptation when no one is looking? When we have financial matters for which we are responsible, how do we handle money when no one is looking? We know everyone works hard when the boss is around, but what do they do when they are not supervised?

In the Parable of the Ten Minas (a *mina* was a sum of money, not a *myna* bird!), Jesus taught the value of doing what is right when the master is away. He spoke of great reward to those who faithfully managed what had been given to their care. "'Well done, my good servant!' his master replied. 'Because you have been trustworthy in a very small matter, take charge of ten cities'" (Luke 19:17).

Jesus also spoke of judgment to those who had not been faithful in doing what they said they would do. "His master replied, 'I will judge you by your own words, you wicked servant!'" (Luke 19:22).

My Uncle Lem, a farmer in Lamont, Tennessee, was absolutely honest in everything he did. When Uncle Lem was ninety years old, he sold his annual crop of tobacco. He received payment by check. When he looked at the check, there was a slight over-payment. Uncle Lem got in his truck and returned the check. The amount was very small, and he was told by an employee of the buyer that he shouldn't have even bothered with it. No one would have missed it

112

or ever known the difference. My Uncle Lem said, "I've been honest all my life, and I'm not going to change now." Shortly after this incident Uncle Lem died—with a clear conscience and his integrity intact.

Ultimately, our concern in always doing right, even when no one is looking, should be the realization that God sees and knows all that we do. It is to Him alone we will give a final accounting of our lives. The writer of Hebrews instructs: "Nothing in all creation is hidden from God's sight. Everything is uncovered and laid bare before the eyes of him to whom we must give account" (Heb. 4:13).

Out of love for and obedience to God we should do what is right. If that isn't reason enough, we should do it out of fear of a holy and just God.

The very night that Daniel interpreted the writing on the wall, the city was invaded by Cyrus. Belshazzar was slain and Darius, the Mede, became king. He appointed 120 administrators over the kingdom. Over these, he appointed three commissioners who reported directly to him. Surprisingly, Daniel, who had served under Nebuchadnezzar and Belshazzar, was one of the three commissioners. This provoked great resentment among the other commissioners; not only because he had also served the enemy, but because he was gaining a reputation for being the most capable and diligent commissioner.

They sought to discredit Daniel, but no matter how hard they tried, no accusation of corruption or negligence could be found. In any period of history, this was rare among political leaders possessing such great power. As a leader, Daniel had the added temptation of abuse or misuse of power. By all indications, he continued to do what was right even when God was blessing his efforts. Daniel was consistently more sensitive and responsive to God's opinions about his place in God's service than to the eyes and evaluations of others in the king's service. He knew self-worth and self-respect come from doing what is right, even when no one sees but God and you.

LESSON 5: PERSEVERE IN WHAT IS RIGHT

What would it take to get you to compromise your integrity? A million dollars? Guaranteed advancement in the corporation of your choice? A life with your dream mate? Being thrown into a den of snarling, man-eating lions?

The disgruntled administrators under Darius' regime wanted to see Daniel fail—any way, at any cost. They devised a scheme to entrap Daniel. These men convinced King Darius to issue a royal decree that no one could pray to any god or man for a period of thirty days. If one prayed during that time, he would be thrown into a lions' den. Of course, Daniel prayed. "Then they said to the king, 'Daniel, who is one of the exiles from Judah, pays no attention to you, O king, or to the decree you put in writing. He still prays three times a day.' When the king heard this, he was greatly distressed; he was determined to rescue Daniel and made every effort until sundown to save him" (Dan. 6:13–14).

The king was forced to abide by his edict. Daniel was taken into custody and led to the lions' den.

What would you have done at this point? Blame your praying on the fact that you didn't know about the edict? Explain that you really weren't praying; rather you were doing a new relaxation/exercise program and only appeared to be praying? Hire a hot-shot attorney from Persia? Confess and promise never to do it again? Or, tell them that you are allergic to cats—especially *big* ones?

Daniel did what he had been doing all along—that which was right in God's eyes. "So the king gave the order, and they brought Daniel and threw him into the lions' den. The king said to Daniel, 'May your God, whom you serve continually, rescue you!'" (Dan. 6:16). And God did.

God sent an angel that gave the lions some severe cases of lockjaw. "The king was overjoyed and gave orders to lift Daniel from out of the den. And when Daniel was lifted from the den no wound was found on him, because he had trusted in God" (Dan. 6:23).

Ron, a fine young businessman, approached me about a difficult situation he was incurring. He had recognized, over a period of time, his supervisor was having an affair with his secretary. The supervisor was now coming to Ron and telling him to lie to help him cover his sexual adventures. This young man was threatened with the loss of his job if he failed to comply.

Ron refused and was fired. The career which he had worked so long in establishing now took a major setback. Ron's security, however, was not in his job. His faith in God was not shaken by this experience, but rather strengthened by his having to rely more completely on God.

Our dens will come. I assure you, each of us will be tested at the point of integrity. For us as Christians, there are no guarantees we will always be rescued from each and every lions' den. Yet we need not fear the snarling lions which try to tear our wholeness apart, for we know that God will be there in the den with us. He will allow us to endure the den. We know for certain, if we persevere in the fight to do what is right, God will overcome the devouring lions in our lives.

Integrity is like a wooden block puzzle. When all the pieces are in place, the puzzle holds together. If you take one piece out, you have to carefully hold it together, or it will all fall apart. So it is with integrity. When piece by piece our integrity is compromised, our wholeness is destroyed. We fall apart.

What we have lost through lapses in our integrity, by God's grace, we can have restored. God is full of mercy and forgiveness, and He is able to make those which are scarlet, white as wool. God wants us to be free, clean and whole—walking in the joy of abundant life. Yet for this to happen there must be a change in perspective. We must see the importance of integrity as God sees it. We must be as committed and as determined as Daniel in maintaining our integrity no matter what happens to us, no matter what we may face. We must have this settled in our minds before we enter the den. We must consistently rely on God to abide with us when things heat up in the furnace. We must desire wholeness and holiness above all else.

CHAPTER EIGHT

OUR PERSPECTIVE OF FAMILY

A high school teacher expressed her concern about two students, a brother and sister, a year apart in age and grade. The boy, a sophomore, was failing in most of his classes. The teacher was not only concerned about his grades but also about his well-being. For months, this young man had progressively become depressed, detached in relationships, and disinterested in all aspects of school. The boy's sister, a freshman, had taken a sudden nose dive in grades. She had begun associating with the wrong crowd, as well as seeking the attention and affection of guys much older than she.

The teacher had called their home on numerous occasions to talk to their single dad. He vowed to hold the kids accountable and to make sure they improved their study habits at home. He constantly referred to grounding them to facilitate improvement in grades and attitudes. After months of trying to help, the teacher finally discovered a big piece of the puzzle that had been missing.

The father, about forty years old and divorced for less than two years, was soon to be married to a nineteen-year-old neighbor. As it turned out, the dad's time and energy were being focused on his new love interest and away from his children. There was a lot of anger and resentment in the home. It's no wonder the kids weren't able to focus on school work; their family was rapidly disintegrating.

THE DISINTEGRATING FAMILY

Some time ago an article entitled "Why the American Family Is in Trouble" appeared in our local newspaper. The author showed great insight on this subject. "The key reason why the American family is in trouble is that too many American husbands and wives consider their families to be of secondary importance. Their number one priority is themselves, their personal growth, fulfillment, and all the other things we say when what we really mean is, 'Me first.' Neither the economic nor the employment status of the parents is the key. What matters is whether the family is at the center of their concern."[1]

The family is at the heart of everything we do and everything we are. Whether we are grandparents, singles, parents, marrieds—whoever we are, our lives revolve around or involve others who are family. Yet despite its importance, the American family has been neglected and desperately needs help. The traditional family is disintegrating in our country.

Over the last thirty years we have seen the deterioration of the family. If you were born after 1955, you may not understand what a traditional family is—or was. When I use the term traditional family, I am referring to a husband and wife, committed to a lifetime of faithful marriage, with children, supported by a network of family who provide a safety net of love and support. It includes the security and commitment of always being able to count on your family being there for you—physically and emotionally—through thick and thin.

Around 1955 things began to change in the lives of the American family. The divorce rate began rising. More mothers took jobs outside the home. The care of children increasingly became the responsibility of others besides the mother. Educational and career advancement saw the transplantation of increasing numbers of Americans to parts of the country away from where their larger family lived. Television, while providing greater communication and entertainment, provided a forum which promoted the declining morality in our country. Sexual liberation came and liberated commitment from the marriage vows of many. In the schools of our nation, relativism and humanism replaced authority and absolutes, the Bible and truth. There also came greater substance abuse—alcohol, prescriptive, and nonprescriptive drugs. A rapid rise and spread of juvenile delinquency came, as well. Abortion

117

and gay rights, formerly two topics one did not discuss in polite company, became the rally cry of a nation in chaos.

Chaos has come to our families. It has ushered in the disintegration of the family. According to the research of George Barna,[2] two out of three children born today will live in a single-parent household. One out of two of those children will be born to unwed parents. More than half of all mothers with children under six years of age are currently in the labor force. There is rising acceptance of a definition of family that differs greatly from that of a traditional family. More than 75 percent of our nation, according to Barna's research, considers an unwed couple, jointly raising children, a family. Slightly more than 25 percent of Americans consider two lesbians or two gays, living with children they are raising, a family.

Many today would argue that there has only been an evolution in our understanding of what a family really is. They believe there has been no significant breakdown in the American family—just a mind shift. I argue that what has become commonly known as "the family" is an inferior hybrid of what God created the family to be.

THE INTEGRATED FAMILY

By integrated, I am not referring to the removal of racial barriers. Instead, I am referring to the removal of barriers or obstacles which keep our families from being whole or complete. Understanding integrated means "made whole or complete," what then is an integrated family? What did God intend for a family to be? For what good purpose did God ordain the family? What are the characteristics of an integrated family?

An integrated family conforms to the purposes for which God ordained the family. What might those purposes be?

PURPOSE 1: THE FAMILY IS TO RAISE CHILDREN

A common reason for marrying is having and raising children; yet, fewer couples are choosing to have children these days. Those who do are having fewer children.[3] Nowadays society tells couples to seek self-fulfillment before being confined by marital or parental commitment and responsibilities. Apparently, many feel that changing diapers and looking after kids cannot bring satisfaction or make contributions the world considers important.

Contrary to the world's message, having children is vitally important. God's mandate to mankind, through His spoken Word to Adam and Eve, was to "be fruitful and increase in number; fill the earth and subdue it" (Gen. 1:28). God blessed the union of man and woman, and then He stated the purpose of their union: child-bearing and "subduing the earth" as a family. It is good to have children. The psalmist sings:

Sons are a heritage from the LORD,
    children a reward from him.
Like arrows in the hands of a warrior
    are sons born in one's youth.
Blessed is the man
    whose quiver is full of them. (Ps. 127:3–5a)

Once again, we need to see children as a gift and a blessing from God, not as a tax advantage or a social disadvantage. We need to view family as holy privilege, not hated sacrifice. We need to be less wrapped up in our lives and more committed to serving others in this God-given role of family. Russell Chandler illustrates the precarious nature of the American family in this story: "Arriving home from work, the harried husband, hand on his forehead, has just realized his ghastly goof. His wife—I'm assuming they're married, although that's a bit risky these days—opens the front door to let him in. 'Great!' she says. 'You remembered to pick up the dinner, but where are the kids?'"[4]

I can relate to that guy. When Jeanette and I married, she was a year and a half from completing her college degree. I promised her dad and God she would get her degree. We postponed her going back to school until we could afford it. By then, we had three young children.

I was pastoring a rapidly growing church, and Jeanette was our church's preschool director. Our children were involved in everything—piano lessons, swimming lessons, gymnastics, and other sports. It took much teamwork to raise the children when she started back with college classes.

Jeanette would get up before daybreak, study for her classes, iron and lay out the children's clothes, then awaken me and pass the baton so she could head to class. I got the kids up, fed them, helped dress them, and delivered them to their respective schools and care giver.

119

I thought I did a pretty good job until the day Jeanette, to her horror, discovered I had sent our daughter, Betsy, to school with her shoes on the wrong feet. I must admit this was not my only goof. There were others that she doesn't know about to this day, but I am reserving those for a deathbed confession, as she might give me a premature "near death" experience if she knew about them! Suffice it to say, we survived it. Together, we raised our family. (And Jeanette graduated cum laude.)

PURPOSE 2: THE FAMILY IS TO PROVIDE A PLACE FOR INDIVIDUAL DEVELOPMENT

The home—not school, not government, not even churches— was intended by God to be the prime place of nurturing and training children. God created the home to be unlike any other place. It has a unique mission: to shelter and provide a loving environment for development of children into capable and Christlike adults. Before there was the church, there was the home. Before there were any schools, there was the home. Before there was government, there was the home. If society as it is today had dictated the progression of creation, I guess it would have had God (excuse me, I mean a Big Bang) first create a bureaucratic government that would have filibustered the feasibility of networking HRS, the school system, and medicine to produce genetically-engineered human prototypes!

There's no place like home to teach our children the skills necessary to survive and be successful in the world. Parents, not a government program or a school course, can provide the best model for mature relationships—with others and with God.

I remember teaching my son to play baseball—as an infielder. The big challenge was teaching him to catch a grounder without turning his head—something my dad had drilled into my head. He began playing Little League and was doing well with what I had taught him; that is, until he nailed the infield umpire with a direct hit to the head in an attempted double play. He sent the 200-plus-pound man flailing in the dirt (a modern-day David and Goliath story). His throw left the umpire's head and pride bruised, the crowd in stitches, and my son bewildered that he—all seventy pounds worth—could strike such a mighty blow. He accomplished what every ballplayer secretly dreams of doing at least once in his lifetime! (I must clarify that I did not teach him this particular fine point of the game.)

To produce individuals who are proficient in life skills takes a great deal of time and loving attention (and some clarification about not hitting slow moving objects!). The home is best suited to provide such a nurturing environment. There children can risk setbacks and failure without fearing ridicule or rejection. There children can be taught to strive for higher, better, and more noble pursuits by parents who only want God's best for them. There children can learn to accept themselves, with God-given limitations, as God's handiwork. There children can develop more wholly and rapidly among devoted family members who are consistently interested in their well-being.

Likewise, in a God-centered home parents, too, can grow as whole individuals. The trust and the commitment of marriage grants freedom to partners to be all God created them to be. The encouragement and support of a spouse can provide the confidence needed to allow God to stretch and shape his or her life according to His design. The love and admiration of a spouse can make the other "leap tall buildings in a single bound"!

PURPOSE 3: THE FAMILY IS TO INSTILL MORALS, VALUES, AND A CHRISTIAN WORLDVIEW

Parents' morals, values, and worldview have a way of being imposed on their children. Their system of beliefs about right and wrong, what's important in life, and what's important in the spiritual realm is shaped in the home. This is the way God planned it.

From earliest Old Testament times, God gave the Abrahamic covenant (see Gen. 22:17–18), which was signified by ceremonial circumcision. The parent, vowing to raise the child according to God's covenant, to love and fear God above all others, and to walk humbly in His ways, would have an eight-day-old son circumcised. In doing so, the parent agreed to raise the child according to God's system of beliefs about the important things in life.

Today, parents still have this God-given responsibility to raise a child in the fear and love of the Lord. How can parents assume such an awesome task? First, parents cannot delegate this responsibility to others: the school, child care, governmental or social agencies, other individuals, or the church. Parents must be parents. They must be on the scene and available for use by God to properly train the child. Second, they must have a personal, saving knowledge of Christ. They must continually seek to understand God's Word and His will in their lives, as well as the child's life.

121

They must be prayerfully committed to raising the child according to biblical principles. Third, both parents must diligently strive to work together in partnership to accomplish this enormous task.

What if your children are grown? Is it too late for you to be a good parent? A fellow preacher told me about his dad's late conversion. The father was antagonistic toward the things of God. He never went to church, never prayed, never read the Bible. At age thirty-two, this dad went to a church service, felt the conviction of the Holy Spirit, and made a profession of faith. My pastor friend told me, "After that experience we started going to church and started reading the Bible. I was just a boy, but I'll never forget the difference in Daddy's life." His dad has since raised two sons who love the Lord and are committed Christians. God can always make a parent (of any age) more effective if that parent puts God first and above all else—even the child, even the spouse.

What if you are a single parent, trying to raise children on your own? Then you really need the love and support of a heavenly Father. It will still be tough, but God can ease your burden. God can give you strength and comfort when you're struggling on your own. When you don't know what to do or say, God can guide you. God can make you a better parent as you seek to impart goodness and truth in the life of your child.

It is imperative that the family regain its rightful place in society. It is imperative that parents once again assume the responsibility of raising their children to be capable adults and impart to them biblical morals and values. It is imperative that the family turn back to God and away from destructive behavioral patterns.

As an individual is to have integrity (or wholeness of being), so, too, must families. Even though times have changed since the days of Ozzie and Harriet, there is still a profound need for integrated families whose strength is measured by their being united as a whole under God, rather than being divided by the world. An integrated family provides a taste of heaven on earth, foreshadowing the family of God.

THE MODEL FAMILY

Is a model family one who manages to stay intact for the lifetime of the marriage partners? Is a model family one with two parents, 2.5 children, one pet, two cars, and a home in the suburbs? Is a model family one whose children never get into any type of trouble?

I am often amused at young parents who are eager to present themselves and their children as the model family. Their marriage is perfect, their children are perfect, and they are perfectly dressed as they drive the perfect car to the perfect school on their way to pursue their perfectly advancing careers. They are the first to let everyone know they have the brightest and the most talented children who are second to none. What happens when the children act like children? What happens when the bottom falls out? Are they less than model if challenges come their way?

I recall a preacher friend telling me about dining in the home of a family who were members of a church where he was the guest evangelist. Seated across the table was a little boy who sat silently during the first half of the meal as he stared at my friend. Now my friend is, by his own admission, a rather large man, so he assumed the child was sizing him up. There was a lapse in the conversation, and in the midst of the silence, the little boy blurted out, "Momma, that preacher is as fat as our old pig!"

While we may not be able to control all that comes out of the mouths of our children, we can regulate some important aspects of their lives. We can strive to build strong God-centered families. How can we do this? In a survey of three thousand families, Dr. Nick Stinnett identified six qualities found in strong families,[5] which I have adapted.

CHARACTERISTIC 1: COMMITMENT TO GOD

A model family begins with two marriage partners who are deeply committed to God through a personal relationship with Jesus Christ as their Lord and Savior. This is foundational in building a family and a home.

Noah and his wife were a couple who were deeply committed to God. The Genesis account records that "Noah was a righteous man, blameless among the people of his time, and he walked with God" (Gen. 6:9). This couple had three sons: Shem, Ham, and Japheth. Although the world at that time was full of corrupt and violent people, God recognized the righteousness and devotion of Noah and established his covenant with Noah, his wife, and his sons and their wives (see v. 18). If they would obey Him, God would protect them from His forthcoming judgment: a flood that was to eradicate life on earth. Noah and his family put their trust in God and did as God instructed them to do. They knew a sure foundation—one on which to build a home (floating or stationary) and one which could weather any storm.

CHARACTERISTIC 2: COMMITMENT TO THE FAMILY

It is heartwarming to see family members who are committed to each other—at all times, in all circumstances, in all ways. Not only is there fidelity between the parents; their is fidelity among all family members. There are few things more damaging to a relationship than having a family member (or spouse) verbally crucify another family member (or spouse) in front of others. Trust and security are violated. The relationship is harmed.

For example, while the world says it is natural and healthy for teens to rebel against their parents, the Bible says all children—and that includes teens—are to honor and obey their parents. Yes, rebellion is natural, but it is also sinful. A child who is a Christian has no business slandering a parent, displaying "an attitude," or defying authority. Likewise, a Christian parent has no business provoking a teen to anger, dishonoring a teen by "running them down" in public or in private, or abusing their authority as parents. Love and mutual respect should be the normative behavior for Christian families.

There needs to be mutual respect for all family members. There must also be mutual support of essential decisions. For instance, a parent may find it necessary to accept a transfer to another city. If the move ultimately benefits the family, it will be necessary for family members not only to adapt to changes, but also to lovingly support each other in this major life decision.

Can you imagine what Mrs. Noah must have thought when her husband said that a great flood was coming to their arid region and their only means of survival would be trusting God and building an ark? Can you imagine the sons trying to convince their wives of the same? What kind of family commitment did it take for Mrs. Noah and especially for the sons to support Mr. Noah in this faith venture? The family ties must have been incredibly strong when Noah and his sons were being ridiculed. Remember, the ridicule lasted for about a century of ark construction before the first drop of rain ever fell. Now, that's commitment!

CHARACTERISTIC 3: GOOD FAMILY COMMUNICATION

Some time ago, my wife went away on a trip. This meant I was forced to come home to a big, empty bed at night. I was feeling awfully lonely and sorry for myself as I turned back the bed covers. To my surprise, there was a note from my bride! Elated, I grabbed it and read, "x o x o x o! Love, Jeanette." I didn't know what she meant. I wondered if it was some code we shared that I had forgotten. As I got ready for bed, I turned the note sideways and upside down to see if I was holding it improperly. I still had no idea what she meant. Maybe it was some exotic way for her to passionately tell me how much she loved me. I lay awake for another ten minutes or so trying to figure it out.

Days later, when she returned, I barely said hello before I was asking her the secret meaning of her note. She said, "Honey, don't you know it means hugs and kisses, hugs and kisses, and more hugs and kisses?" I looked dumbfounded as I replied, "I have never seen it written like that before! Never in my life." We had a good laugh over the miscommunication. (I don't know what I will do if she writes me a note with z's and w's on it!)

Good communication is important in any relationship. It is critical for family members to effectively communicate with each other. I am not just referring to being good talkers; I am also referring to being good listeners. Husbands, fathers, are you paying attention? Family members need to feel that others truly are interested in what they are saying. Also, they need the freedom to communicate without criticism. To work together as an effective team, the family must communicate.

The Noah family must have been awesome communicators. Can you imagine? First, they had to listen to God's plans. They then had to follow His plans by working together to get everything done before it started raining. I think about all the times I have forgotten to pick up something a family member needed from the store because I didn't listen, didn't write it down, or forgot my list. The Noah family must have had some incredible shopping lists!

To build something as huge as the ark took working together, formulating plans, and assigning tasks. Then, when they had to round up all the animals, suppose they failed to communicate and ended up with ten squirrels, sixteen foxes, and no rabbits! Effective communication was essential to their survival—and to the rest of God's creations.

CHARACTERISTIC 4: TIME SPENT TOGETHER

An area where commitment is greatly needed among family members is the consistent commitment of time. Quality time is not enough for children; they also need great quantities of time. It is like oxygen. You have to have a certain amount of it to live. The less you have, the poorer your quality of life. Possessions, vacations, and careers cannot be primary for parents. Again, let me say, children need the time and attention of their parents. There is no substitute for a parent's time.

Families need time to enjoy each other. It may take some planning to coordinate the schedules of busy parents and children, but families must have meals together and other times to relax and recreate together.

I laugh when I think about Noah and his family. Time is one thing they certainly had as they were cooped up on that boat together for over a year! I wonder what they did. Wallaby races on the Promenade Deck? Cow pod shuffleboard on the Atlantic Deck? Penguin bowling on the Caribbean Deck? Maybe a game of "Go Fish" for eight? I guess they couldn't catch up on their reading because there's no indication of written language. Perhaps they dreamed about their future and shared plans for that mountain hideaway.

CHARACTERISTIC 5: ABILITY TO SOLVE PROBLEMS IN A CRISIS

Life brings its crises—traumatic illness, death of loved one, loss of job. A crisis can tear a family apart or knit it more closely together. A family that upholds each other in a time of crisis can turn a crisis into a life challenge they face and handle together— with God's help. There is nothing like the support of a loving family in offering counsel, solutions, and encouragement.

It has been said that in a lifetime we have only twenty-five to thirty close friends, including our immediate family and relatives. They are our earthly network of support when a crisis comes. If we do not have this network, to whom can we turn and on whom can we rely when a crisis comes?

Noah's family faced a crisis of major proportion. They had an earthly network of eight. They relied on each other in offering solutions and encouragement when they faced adversity. They weren't boat builders; they were farmers (Gen. 9:20), but build a huge boat they did. It actually floated and didn't leak (too badly). They had to corral all those animals and then get them on board. They had to store enough food for everyone and every animal. When the rains stopped, they figured out the system of sending out the birds. It was a good system, and they were able to step out on dry land. This family was most definitely solutions oriented. That's what kept them afloat.

CHARACTERISTIC 6: EXPRESSIVE OF MUTUAL APPRECIATION

We all need expressions of affirmation and praise, expressions of love and appreciation. Children have this need. Adults have this need. The family, in particular, has this need. Yet, one of the easiest things for family members to do is to overlook saying thank you to each other. We try to instill in our children the habit of saying please and thank you. Somewhere along the line we get busy or preoccupied and forget expressions of appreciation. More tragic than this, we often offer more negative expressions, such as criticism, than we do positive expressions to our loved ones.

A study by Dr. Lacy Hall[6] traced verbal input—positive and negative—received at home, at work, at school, etc., by those being studied over a year and a half. Every detail of the day was recorded. Results showed 90 percent of all input received during the course of the day was negative! While this may be true out in the world, we must ask ourselves if these statistics hold true in our home?

Family members need to express love and appreciation freely. Sincere compliments and praise are important to developing a sense of well-being—especially in the home. The goal of genuine expressions of appreciation should be to build each other up in Jesus Christ.

I wonder how the Noah family felt when they finally landed on dry land? The Bible gives us a clue. We are told Noah and his family came out of the ark. "Then Noah built an altar to the LORD and, taking some of all the clean animals and clean birds, he sacrificed burnt offerings on it" (Gen. 8:20). With a heart full of gratitude and thanksgiving, Noah worshiped God in this oblation of praise. Noah and his family expressed their profound appreciation to God.

As I think about this special family, they truly are the model family—the only family on earth God chose to preserve. They must have been an incredible bunch. As far as expressing their appreciation to one another, I am certain they did. There is no way on God's green earth—or on His blue waters—they could have faced this challenge without a healthy appreciation for each other. When the waters were surging, the storms were raging, and the ark was being tossed about, they had only each other—and God.

127

When it was all over, I can imagine Shem telling his children story upon story about Uncle Japheth's courage in the Great Flood!

Like all families, even this model family had some problems. Noah's son, Ham, expressed ridicule—instead of appreciation—for his dad (Gen. 9:20–23). This was not acceptable in their family and he faced severe judgment for doing so (see v. 25). The other two sons, however, received Noah's blessing, the highest form of appreciation a father could give (see vv. 26–27).

THE FAMILY OF GOD

As you think about Noah's family and God saving them above all others, do you think God would do the same for you and your family? Would the righteousness of your family be comparable to that of Noah's family? Based on this, would your family merit salvation?

Your family may be considered a model family by all who know you; however, "there is no one righteousness, not even one" who merits such favor from God (Rom. 3:10). The salvation of your family—and mine—is dependent on the merit of what God alone has done through Jesus Christ. The good news is God offers adoption to all who are united to His Son in faith! While your family or mine is not righteous enough to merit His favor, God the Father chooses to adopt those who are justified through Christ's death and resurrection as His sons and daughters. Our adoption into the family of God is grounded in grace.

> Praise be to the God and Father of our Lord Jesus Christ, who has blessed us in the heavenly realms with every spiritual blessing in Christ. For he chose us in him before the creation of the world to be holy and blameless in his sight. In love he predestined us to be adopted as his sons through Jesus Christ, in accordance with his pleasure and will—to the praise of his glorious grace, which he has freely given us in the One he loves. In him we have redemption through his blood, the forgiveness of sins, in accordance with the riches of God's grace that he lavished on us with all wisdom and understanding. (Eph. 1:3–8)

Being adopted in the family of God provides the benefits of eternal safety and security. We need not fear for "we are heirs—heirs of God and co-heirs with Christ, if indeed we share in his sufferings in order that we may also share in his glory" (Rom. 8:17). Sonship, as demonstrated by Jesus Christ, comes with a price.

Jesus paid for our adoption with His blood. Christ's suffering is the basis and the model of our sonship.[7] Our adoption into the family of God demands obedience to the Father's will. Living with the Father requires living like the Father.

We, as God's children, are not left on our own to raise ourselves. In the four references[8] to Christian adoption in the New Testament, the Holy Spirit is always mentioned. The Holy Spirit is the Spirit of the Father and of the Son. The Spirit makes us heirs. He provides that family bond. He protects us and guides us. He rears us to resemble our Elder Brother, Jesus Christ. Through Him we are able to cry out, "Abba, Father" (Gal. 4:6).

For those whose earthly families have been less than model families and whose family members have brought pain into their lives, being able to cry out to the Heavenly Father is incredibly comforting and reassuring. There is a Father on whom they can depend. There is a familial relationship on which they can count. For the broken and hurt who respond in saving faith, the greatest blessing of all awaits—that is, being adopted into the family of God.

There is a poignant story of an adoption, of sorts, of a puppy by a little boy. A store owner was posting a sign, Puppies For Sale, just as a young boy entered his shop. "How much are you going to sell the puppies for?" he asked.

"Anywhere from thirty to fifty dollars," the store owner replied.

"I have $2.37," the little boy said as he pulled some change out of his pocket. "May I look at them?"

The store owner smiled and whistled for the mother dog, who came running down the store aisle followed by five tiny balls of fur. One puppy was lagging far behind the rest. Immediately the little boy singled out the lagging, limping puppy and said, "What's wrong with that little dog?"

The store owner explained that the little puppy didn't have a hip socket and would always limp. The little boy became excited. "That's the puppy I want to buy!"

"No, you don't want to buy that little dog," the store owner said. "If you really want him, I'll just give him to you."

The little boy looked quite upset as he said to the store owner, "I don't want you to give him to me. That little dog is worth every bit as much as all the other dogs and I'll pay full price. In fact, I'll give you $2.37 now, and 50¢ a month until I have paid for him."

"You don't really want to buy this little dog," the store owner countered. "He's never going to be able to run and jump and play with you like the other puppies."

To this, the little boy reached down and rolled up his pant leg to reveal a badly twisted, crippled left leg supported by a big metal brace. He looked up at the store owner and replied, "Well, I don't run so well myself, and the little puppy will need someone who understands!"[9]

Like the crippled little puppy, we, in our spiritually handicapped condition, need a loving family into which we can be adopted and from whom we can draw healing strength. We need a Father who understands our frailties and loves us in spite of our sad shape. We need acceptance and security which is only found in the family of God.

Adoption into His family brings hope. Adoption into His family brings validation for our existence. Adoption into His family is the ultimate in relationships and support. We are no longer left on our own to fend for ourselves. As the privileged heirs to His throne, our perspective of life—including life as a part of earthly families—dramatically changes. We no longer have to limp through life. We have the power of the King, our Father, to radically change our world. What a perspective!

With this perspective, we should be challenged to seek to bring a little heaven to earth in the way we relate to our family members and in the way we witness to the world through our home life. God has chosen to bless us by giving us earthly families. As God's children, we need to maximize this incredible blessing in our homes. It should be obvious to all who the Patriarch of our family is. Our respect for His authority and guidance should never be questioned in the way we live.

Family life—earthly and spiritual—is God's provision for those He loves.

CHAPTER NINE

OUR PERSPECTIVE OF FRIENDSHIP

I chuckled as I picked up a fellow pastor's "Fourth Annual Christmas Greetings Form Letter" to his friends. I thought, *What a title—and statement of our times! To stay close to our loved ones, we've become obliged to produce an annual report, accounting for our previous year's life. This form letter then releases us from any obligation for further personal contact for the duration of one year!* It was more than Wilson's letter's title, however, that grabbed my attention. His closing paragraph sums up another common sentiment: "I celebrated my 50th birthday in November, so I joined AARP. I am looking forward to the second half of my life."

I could relate to Wilson's response to his milestone birthday. The big four-O, five-O, or six-O birthday seems to demand some response, some course of action. For him, it was his resignation to join AARP and his optimistic determination to make the last half of his life count. For others the response might be doing something about their physical appearance or mode of transportation. Still others might dwell on their accomplishments or failures.

ASSESSING FRIENDS IN LIFE

The turning point for me came at age forty-five. You see, when I hit forty, I had just become pastor of First Baptist Church in Orlando. Things were moving so rapidly that special events in my

131

ministry and my family life seemed to pass by in a flurry of activity. Now that I think about it, almost the entire time of my thirties and forties is a blur! It was not until I turned forty-five that it hit me—I was heading into the second half of life!

Bob Buford said that in the first half of your life you are trying to be successful, but after half-time, you begin to think about being significant.[1] Birthdays, anniversaries, New Year's Day—all serve as reminders to stop and take inventory of one's life. At forty-five, I did just that. That particular inventory changed the way I looked at what matters in my life.

I try now to take my vacations in longer segments, rather than brief getaways. I need the extra time to be quiet, to listen to God, and to think. Some of these times, I just sit with no particular mental agenda, trying only to be quiet on the inside. It is then that I can more keenly discern God's direction in my life. I am better able to focus on my relationship to God and on my usefulness in His kingdom work.

During these times I also reflect on my relationships with family and friends. Prioritizing and reevaluating whether my words of commitment mesh with my calendared commitments are essential to my remaining true to God and those people that I love. After these vacations, I am refreshed and committed to make more significant investments in the lives of those who are important to me. I am determined, upon returning to my routine, to spend more time with my family and friends.

Even for a person who is seldom given to such introspection, turning forty (-five) or fifty often makes one stop and think. A story is told of a guy who was celebrating his fortieth birthday by having dinner with his wife, Darcy. He was unusually quiet that evening. As they were waiting for their food to arrive, he passed the napkin on which he had been doodling over to his wife.

"Darcy, what does that look like?"

"Well," she said, "it looks like a casket."

"Yeah, that's right," he said. He went on to ask, "If I were to die tomorrow, who would be my pallbearers?"

Darcy did not like the thought and wondered if there was something that Tim was not telling her.

"Just think about it for a minute. How many people does it take to carry a casket?"

"Well, usually six," Darcy replied, eyeing her husband curiously.

"Which six of my friends would you ask to be pallbearers?" As Darcy was thinking, Tim elaborated on the criteria: "I'm not talking about the acquaintances and associates who would do it if they didn't have an important appointment. I'm talking about the friends that would drop everything to drop me."[2] His concern hits home for all of us at some point.

I remember my dad talking about an old man who was the wealthiest person in Robertson County, Tennessee. He had everything materially one could want; however, the one thing he did not possess was friends. In all of his acquiring, he had failed to invest in meaningful relationships. When he died, they had to pay people to be his pallbearers. Here was a guy who seemingly had it all, but in reality he had little that was of true value.

Stop and think. When was the last time you took a personal inventory of the people who would drop everything on your account? Is your list lacking like that of a mother of two teens who was troubled by her failure to stop long enough to cultivate relationships while managing the demands of motherhood. She woke up one day to the realization she had alienated herself—unintentionally—from those friends who could be a significant part of her life long after her teens left the nest. Her plight is not all that uncommon.

I find this particularly true of men. Some studies show that "for the American male, only ten percent have real friends."[3] For men, it is not that hard to come by acquaintances, casual relationships, or even guys with whom you "hang out." The difficulty, however, lies in making a real committed-forever, I'd-lay-my-life-down-for-you friend. Alan Loy McGinnis commented on this in his best-selling book *The Friendship Factor:* "Since so few males have been allowed the luxury of openness and vulnerability in a relationship, they are not aware of the gaping void in their emotional lives. In short, they don't know what they are missing."[4]

McGinnis went on to cite a study by British sociologist, Marion Crawford:

> [Crawford] found that middle-aged men and women had considerably different definitions of friendship. By an overwhelming margin, women talked about trust and confidentiality, while men described a friend as "someone I go out with" or "someone whose company I enjoy." For the most part, men's friendships revolve around activities while women's revolve around sharing. A man will describe as "my very good friend" a person who is an occasional tennis partner or someone he just met five minutes ago.[5]

POSSESSING FRIENDS FOR LIFE

While some men and women may have a difficult time in cultivating close friendships, I believe these relationships are well worth the effort and are among life's greatest blessings. John and Terry are two men who know the value of true friendship. They have been friends for over thirty years.

These two born-again husbands and fathers have known each other since the days of early manhood in their native Great Britain. For ten years, John, a native of Wales, was a pastor in Portsmouth, England. During that time John and Terry were involved in many exciting escapades together. They both participated in numerous evangelistic youth outreaches in England. They also worked together in missions, driving trucks in and out of Poland during the Solidarity Labor Union strikes.

"During those four years in which we carried hundreds of thousands of pounds of medical and relief supplies in and out of the Warsaw Pact nations," said Terry, "the Lord kept us safe and miraculously supplied our needs."

"During one of those trips to Poland," John continued, "when we were driving along in -20° below weather, we dreamed up the idea of going into business together. Ten years ago we formed a business with a hundred British pounds and willing hands. Today we employ 700 people in Great Britain."

"What does friendship mean to John and me?" was Terry's rhetorical question. "It means everything! We committed ourselves to each other and have lived with that covenant for over thirty years."

"Terry and I are honest and transparent with each other," John added. "We regularly pray for each other. We seek God's will together and submit to Him and each other in major decisions. We have sought each year to do something meaningful for God. We are accountable to each other, we believe in each other, and, above all, we are *proud* to be friends!"

Relationally speaking, some people just naturally fit together—like country ham and biscuits. From the first time they meet each other, they click. In the Bible, Jonathan and David were two such friends whose friendship transcended every social division and endured every imaginable test. Most of us know that Jonathan and David were friends, but what we may not know is *why* they were friends. To understand what drew them together, we have to go back to an earlier time in Jonathan's life.

The Philistines had subjugated Israel for years until, under the leadership of Samuel, the oppressors were driven out. Immediately after regaining their freedom, the people demanded of Samuel that they be given a king to fight their battles for them.

It was not long after Saul had been anointed king of Israel that Jonathan, his son, went out and "smote" a garrison of the Philistines. This attack so provoked their arch enemy that they assembled a great army at a place called Michmash to come again against Israel. The invading army was so vast it was compared to the sand of the sea.

The people of Israel had no weapons because the Philistines had done away with all the blacksmiths. There were only two swords in Israel. Saul had one, and Jonathan had the other. Most of the men, who had been summoned to Saul at Gilgal, were now scattering to hide in any place they could find. Saul was terrified and foolishly offered the burnt offering because he grew impatient waiting for Samuel.

Seeing all that was going on around him, Jonathan said to his armor-bearer, "I've got an idea. Let's go over and attack the Philistines. Perhaps the Lord will work for us, for the Lord can win with many or with few" (see 1 Sam. 14:6).

The response of his armor-bearer: "Go for it. I'm right behind you."

So they went down to the pass defended by the Philistines who were encamped high above on the cliffs of Bozez and Seneh. Jonathan and his armor-bearer climbed up and engaged a garrison of Philistines.

When they got to the top of that rock, the bloody battle which ensued on the half-acre plateau left twenty Philistines dead at the hand of Jonathan and his armor-bearer. Confusion broke out in the Philistine camp, the men of Israel rallied, and a great battle was won for Saul that day.

Talk about a man! Jonathan stood out among all the others as a tough, courageous warrior who had remarkable confidence in God.

In the years that followed, Saul was continually engaged in battles with the neighboring nations—the Moabites, the Ammonites, the Edomites, the Amalekites, and, of course, the Philistines. A few years after they were defeated at Michmash, the armies of the Philistines and the armies of Saul were facing each other again, each occupying high ground with a valley in between. The Philistines sent out a nine-foot giant as their champion to challenge Israel.

"Then the Philistine said, 'This day I defy the ranks of Israel! Give me a man and let us fight each other'" (1 Sam. 17:10).

All the men of Israel were terrified, as they were at Michmash. The daily challenge went unanswered until one day David, on an errand to the battlefield for his father, went out to confront Goliath. The giant was knocked out cold by a rock to the forehead from David's .38 caliber slingshot. The shepherd boy ran up and cut the giant's head off with his own sword. The men of Israel cheered wildly, pursued the Philistines, and won a great battle. Abner, the commander of Saul's army, found David, with Goliath's bloody head still in hand, and brought him before Saul and Jonathan. "After David had finished talking with Saul, Jonathan became one in spirit with David, and he loved him as himself" (1 Sam. 18:1).

Not everyone is as blessed as these two men in connecting with a friend for life. I believe it is something most desire, but many—especially men—find it hard to attain. Madison Avenue realizes and acknowledges this. Just think about the way they choose to market products, such as beer. Beer commercials are directed, not so subtly, at men and promise two things: beautiful women and meaningful friendships with other guys who share a common gusto for life. Sitting around the campfire together they say, "It just doesn't get any better than this!" The reason these guy-commercials are so designed is the advertising agencies know men are looking for those kinds of relationships, but very few have them. We have a hard time finding people with whom we can relate on a deep level.

A young businessman talked to me about this difficulty. In his search for meaningful relationships, he initiated stopping at a local bar on his way home after work. He began this practice after seeing all the cars parked outside the bar, assuming this was an indicator that people had found something special on the inside. Soon he realized those on the inside were not finding that for which they searched. They all were merely assembled there, looking for what so few of them would ever find. Some time later, this man's search led him to Jesus. In Christ, he found the one meaningful relationship which would color and shape all other relationships. He needed the bar scene no more.

When Jonathan saw what David did, he suddenly met a young man like himself. Perhaps Jonathan had looked all over Israel for a man who matched him in heart and mind. Perhaps he was as frustrated as some today because of the lack of meaningful friendships. But even though he was from the opposite end of the socioeconomic spectrum, as soon as he saw David, he instantly reached out in friendship.

BUILDING BLOCKS OF TRUE FRIENDSHIP

Jonathan and David had something very special, a relationship which became one of the most consistent and defining aspects of their lives. What does it take to cultivate such a relationship?

BUILDING BLOCK 1: COMMON OUTLOOK, COMMON GOALS

"After David had finished talking with Saul, Jonathan became one in spirit with David, and he loved him as himself" (1 Sam. 18:1).

Jonathan identified with something he saw in David and instantly sought to become friends with him. They were both courageous warriors who were willing to proceed against all odds based solely on their confidence in God. You can't get that kind of camaraderie in just any acquaintance! The bond shared by David and Jonathan was not to be found among those who had hidden from the Philistines at Michmash nor those who trembled at the sight of Goliath.

There is something about sharing a vision and working together for a common cause that supplies one of those building blocks for true friendship. This is one of the aspects of Terry's and John's relationship that has made it strong and rich. They've always looked for ways to serve the Lord together. Whether it is driving relief trucks behind the Iron Curtain or leading in youth evangelism, they make it a mutual concern and yearly goal to share in service to God.

Finding a friend who shares your world- and lifeview is an important basis on which to build a relationship. Finding a friend with whom you can share a vision, your passion for life, is a most desirable building block! If you want this kind of relationship, get involved in doing great things for the Lord. It doesn't matter so much what it is—working on the church building, teaching the second grade Sunday school class, working with the homeless, or going on a challenging mission trip. Just step out in faith and ask God to give you a soul mate with a kindred spirit alongside whom you can serve Him.

Such a prayer was answered for a Christian businesswoman named Janis. She had prayed for a true friend. God answered her prayer early one morning. Janis was late in catching a 6:20 A.M. Labor Day flight several years ago. She made it to the gate just in time for her departure. She rushed on board and hurriedly found her seat. Someone else was mistakenly seated there. The mistake was cleared up, the woman moved over to the middle seat, and Janis was seated in her assigned aisle seat.

Janis noticed that the woman seated next to her was reading a book about Christianity and fasting. She thought, *Great! This woman is a Christian. There's no wedding band, so she must be single like me. There's a good chance she's from my hometown. Maybe I should talk to her. We might have some things in common.* Janis never said a word to the woman; instead, she closed her eyes and took a nap.

Tuesday night, Janis headed to the kick-off for a new year of a community Bible study group. The hundred or so women were seated in assigned groups of fifteen. As Janis was seated, the woman from the airplane also took a seat in Janis's group. They both recognized each other, shared names and significant information; there was an instantaneous bonding—like the bonding between Jonathan and David. They had much in common. Their friendship was established. Both felt God had ordained their meeting and their friendship. Over time their friendship grew to the point they felt like sisters. Janis's prayer was answered.

BUILDING BLOCK 2: COMMITMENT OF LIFE, COVENANT OF LOVE

"And Jonathan made a covenant with David because he loved him as himself. Jonathan took off the robe he was wearing and gave it to David, along with his tunic, and even his sword, his bow and his belt" (1 Sam. 18:3–4).

This covenant of love was binding between these two men. They were so serious about their commitment that they took an oath before the Lord, much like the exchanging of wedding vows! In the face of adversity and personal sacrifice, Jonathan supported his friend—in protecting David from Saul's rage and even in acknowledging the throne should be David's and not his. Jonathan's commitment did not waver his entire life.

In 2 Samuel, David's care of Jonathan's crippled son Mephibosheth (see 9:1–11; 21:7), after Jonathan's death, shows David's commitment to the relationship never faltered either. We see in their relationship another key building block to true friendship: unwavering, unconditional commitment to the other person. This sounds somewhat foreign in today's selfish, throw-away society.

Everyone would love to have that kind of friend, but one would not want to make that kind of pledge flippantly. The cost can be great, for it demands self-sacrifice and loving-one's-neighbor-more-than-self commitment. This kind of covenant relationship, like a marriage, will grow stronger over the years as friends love and serve each other.

Janis and Kelly understood this type of commitment. Over the course of their friendship, Janis discovered she had breast cancer. Her dear friend, Kelly, saw her through her treatments and recovery. Kelly later needed Janis in a time of personal difficulties involving job struggles, and Janis was there for her. They consistently stuck by each other. Their friendship grew even more precious, like the friendship of Jonathan and David.

BUILDING BLOCK 3: CONSTRUCTIVE ENCOURAGEMENT, CONSISTENT WORDS OF SUPPORT

"And Saul's son Jonathan went to David at Horesh and helped him find strength in God. 'Don't be afraid,' he said. 'My father Saul will not lay a hand on you. You will be king over Israel, and I will be second to you. Even my father Saul knows this.' The two of them made a covenant before the LORD. Then Jonathan went home, but David remained at Horesh" (1 Sam. 23:16–18).

Again, Jonathan's commitment called for putting David's needs and aspirations before his own. I repeat this thought because it contains another essential building block to true friendship: the constant need for words of encouragement and support. Note how Jonathan's acts of commitment were accompanied by words of encouragement. Who else can better lift our spirit than a dear friend? Whose words can we trust more than a true friend's? Who else cares enough to focus his or her conversation on us rather than on him- or herself than a real friend?

Janis, in telling about her friend, said the thing which knitted them more closely together was a time when Kelly needed encouragement about a failed relationship. Early one Sunday morning she called Janis. Janis could tell immediately something was quite wrong. Responding to her friend's need, Janis went over to her home. Janis said they talked and cried the entire day, from early morning until late evening. Their relationship was sealed. Janis was the person to whom Kelly turned in her time of need. Janis responded as a true friend. They became friends for life.

Fellowship with God often deepens as a result of fellowship with one another. It has been said one of the most important factors in determining your future is your choice of friends. We tend to become more and more like the people with whom we associate because they are like mirrors to our own lives. We see and evaluate ourselves in the reflection and words of our friendships. Apart from the fellowship of godly and mature friends, the quality of your faith, your witness, your thoughts, your words, and your behavior can gradually deteriorate without your notice. Caution: choose your friends wisely because they become the inspiration for you to become a greater or a lesser person.

STUMBLING BLOCKS TO TRUE FRIENDSHIP

Had Jonathan not gone with his feelings and pursued a friendship with David the outcome could have been quite different in both of their lives! Had Jonathan and David failed in any of the following ways their friendship and their very lives would have taken drastically different courses. Here are several stumbling blocks that will hinder the productive development of friendship.

STUMBLING BLOCK 1: FAILURE TO SHOW TRUE FEELINGS

It is important to sincerely let another know how we truly feel when pursuing a relationship. There's a certain element of risk involved in initiating a friendship. Rejection is possible. You probably know the routine. John and Mary casually get to know Dick and Jane in their Sunday school class. They seem to have common interests. John and Mary comment to each other that it would be nice to get to know Dick and Jane better. Since they don't have mutual friends who might get them together, John and Mary must initiate the relationship if anything's going to happen. Should they casually invite Dick and Jane to join them for a meal after church? Or should they be bold, telephone Dick and Jane, and invite them over for dinner?

Mary tries to pass the buck to John by commenting, "You're much better at talking to new people than I, so you call."

To which John adeptly responds, "But, Dear, it might seem impolite for anyone other than the hostess to do the inviting!"

Who's going to make the first move? In the story of Jonathan and David, it was Jonathan who made the first move. He was the one who risked rejection to initiate a relationship with a guy he thought could be a friend.

Beyond initiating a relationship by showing one's interest, it is imperative for one to continue to let his or her true feelings show throughout the relationship. Honesty is the best policy! This doesn't come easily to everyone. I find that men often have a problem in this area.

I was with a group of men who were discussing the challenges they face in life. Many commented about how their fathers never hugged or kissed them. It wasn't that their dads didn't love them, but their dads were uncomfortable with physical displays of emotions. In fact, the group at large could not even remember their grandfathers showing them affection in this manner.

In my early life I never saw or experienced much masculine display of emotion because most of the men in my family just didn't do that. The males in my family might hug, awkwardly, without the show of strong affection. Into my manhood, things began to change. My dad and I began exchanging hugs as we got older. This happened as I overcame some of the insecurities that I thought all men were *supposed* to have. The more I became secure in who I was in Christ, the more I began to appreciate the way God had filled me with His love to show affection and emotion to others. It took some overcoming, but the results have been worth the risk.

My son and daughters are very affectionate, and we enjoy a great emotional freedom with each other. The same is true of my relationship with my precious wife. This has spilled over into my other personal relationships and into my ministry. I have found that people need a display of genuine emotion—a hug or a word of sincere encouragement. For a true friendship, it is essential. A lack of true emotional support is a stumbling block to significant relationships.

STUMBLING BLOCK 2: USE OF OTHERS FOR PERSONAL GAIN

Some people look at relationships only in terms of how it will improve their business or social goals. Lewis shared a disappointing experience with me. He began attending a rather large church when he moved into the Central Florida area. Typically, his wife made friends quickly, but it was not so easy for him. Previously he had long-term friendships; but the new job forced this move, and he was having to start all over. He met other men in the church and went through the routine: "What's your name? Where do you work? How many kids do you have and how old are they? What

141

do you do in your spare time?" This was his way of searching for some kind of link that would help him build a relationship. Nothing, however, seemed to click with the men he met. Those whom he liked seemed to have an already long list of friends.

Every Sunday morning at a prescribed time in the order of worship, the pastor of his new church asked everyone to stand up, greet one another, and introduce themselves to anyone they didn't know. Lewis complied to avoid his wife's disapproval, but doubted that this formality was, as the pastor proclaimed, certain proof that they were a "friendly church." One Sunday morning he greeted a man sitting on the same row. In that brief moment he felt a kindred spirit. That morning, after the auditorium cleared, the two men stayed behind, resting on the pews, and talked.

Maybe this is one of the guys I have been looking for, Lewis began to think.

Then the bubble burst.

It suddenly became obvious what was really happening here. The guy who had seemed so genuinely interested in a friendship only wanted someone else to be involved in his multi-level marketing business! Feeling disgusted and a little defrauded, Lewis excused himself and headed for the car. From that point on, he and his wife went to church increasingly late and left immediately. Shortly afterward, they quit going altogether.

Men and women alike often approach relationships in a way that is too self-indulgent. "What is in this relationship for me?" "What benefit can I get for all my time, money, and effort invested in this relationship?" Today "doing lunch" usually includes an agenda to accomplish something or to "be in the know" with the "right people." All too rarely in today's society does one share a meal just to enjoy and maintain a friendship. Consequently, many are missing out on long-term relationships simply because of misplaced priorities.

Jonathan carefully ordered his priorities in his friendship with David. Rather than being self-seeking, he was self-sacrificing in their relationship. Failure on his part to do so would have been a stumbling block to their enjoying a lifetime of brotherhood.

STUMBLING BLOCK 3: COMPETITION RATHER THAN TEAMWORK

There is nothing which binds people together like being on a team; struggling and sacrificing together to win the championship, to be successful, to reach a goal. In today's business world the struggle to get a step up on the corporate ladder often means stepping on other people in the process. Sometimes the greater sense of competition comes not from the other company, but from the coworker who is trying to make points with the boss to get ahead of you. A lot of men and women have found that being friendly, open, and honest with coworkers—a "team player"—have resulted in their being passed over for promotions.

Christians should be sincere and straightforward in their relationships, without any hidden agendas. The character of Christ is to *serve others* to lift them up, not *use others* as stepping stones for personal advancement. Co-laborers, not competitors, should be the goal in relationships. This was characteristic of Jonathan's and David's relationship. Jonathan was never gripped by the jealousy of David that so consumed his father. Instead, he did all within his power to assure the well-being of his beloved friend.

Competition, which thrives in the corporate world, has found its way into ministerial circles. I received a letter from a man who pastored a sister Baptist church in our city. I had always been friendly with him, but he had responded coolly toward me. I tried everything I could to break through this barrier, but to no avail. I had not seen him for a while when I received his letter.

In the letter, he asked me to forgive him. He went on to explain, "I had resented you and God's blessings upon your ministry. Out of that resentment, I had become jealous and did not want to be around you. It seemed unfair for you to be so blessed and for me not to be as blessed." He continued, "Recently I have come down with a critical illness that has caused me to stop and reevaluate my life. In doing so, the Holy Spirit showed me that I had a wrong spirit toward you. I have confessed my sin to God and asked for His forgiveness. Now I am writing you to ask you for your forgiveness. I do love you, Jim, and appreciate your ministry. I am sorry I was so petty and jealous in the way I responded to your overtures. I do hope we can be closer brothers in the future."

God changed the perspective of this pastor in such a wonderful way. He could see me as a friend, not as an enemy. Through focusing on relationship building, he was able to see me as a colaborer, not as a competitor. We now do our Father's work more effectively as brothers in Christ.

TAKING STEPS TOWARD
BUILDING TRUE FRIENDSHIPS

Friendships are an essential part of what makes life the best it can be. With enough good friends, you can get through almost anything. Without meaningful friendships, even the best of times are hollow and empty. If you don't presently have these close relationships, here are several simple steps which may help you change your perspective and help you in building a relationship.

First, ask God to give you at least one real friend. "Give me a friend with whom I can knit my spirit and my heart. Give me a demonstration of Your type of love and loyalty in a friend. I want a true friend in my life."

Second, choose someone you'd like to imitate in the way they relate to others and reflect God. This is someone about whom you think, *Boy, I'd like to get to know that person. I'd like to be called his (or her) friend, and I'd like to be more like him (or her).* Choose your friends wisely. "He who walks with the wise grows wise" (Prov. 13:20). Over time you will find yourself becoming more like those whom you choose to imitate and call your friends.

Third, we get real friends by initiating the hunger for friendship. At first, you may find that your desired friend might seem uninterested in a relationship; however, with careful attention you can probably plant in them the desire to get to know you better. With that, you're on your way!

We all need friends who love and care enough for us that they are willing to ask the hard questions, who don't backpedal and look for someone else to be near when we begin to share difficult problems. We all need friends with whom we can be completely honest, knowing they will tell us the truth even if it hurts.

Friendship is expensive. It requires a costly investment of your life and energy if the friendship is to be a lifetime friendship. As God changes your perspective, you will become someone others will desire to call their friend. Practice befriending others. Know for certain a good friend can be one of your most valuable possessions and, most certainly, should be treasured among the very best things in life.

PART THREE

SHARPENING OUR PERSPECTIVE

CHAPTER TEN

OUR PERSPECTIVE OF JOY

My friend and brother in the ministry, David Ring, was born with cerebral palsy and faced formidable challenges because of his physical condition. Surviving insurmountable obstacles became a way of life for David. Many events in the life of his family were catastrophic. David's three brothers were born hemophiliacs and died young from disease-related causes. In fact, one died of AIDS after receiving a disease-tainted transfusion. His dad lost an arm in a farming accident. Poverty engulfed their family. David's parents' marriage failed. As if that separation were not enough, both of his parents were taken from him in death while David was still a schoolboy. Suffice it to say, David has known his fair share of adversity.

Likewise, David's spiritual rebirth has caused him to know a generous share of God's blessing. David's conversion brought him a new life in Jesus Christ. The indwelling and enabling Holy Spirit allowed David to experience true joy in being the special person God created him to be. David, now a nationally acclaimed evangelist, says of this joy, "Every child of God receives joy at the time of his new birth. The second trait of the Spirit is joy, according to Galatians 5:22. I'm not talking about happiness. Happiness and joy are totally different. Happiness comes and goes, but joy comes and stays. Happiness is determined by circumstances, but joy depends on our relationship with the Lord Jesus. Your happiness can be taken away because of circumstances, but nobody can remove your joy."[1]

David, rather than feeling bitter and discouraged, feels peace and confidence in God's purpose for the circumstances of his life. "We live down in the dumps because we're looking at our circumstances the wrong way. If I looked at my shaky body or my limitations, you'd better believe I would be down in the dumps. But the key is, view your situation not as a handicap but as a blessing of God or a tool He can use. Thank God, I don't look at cerebral palsy. I look at what God does in my life, and it becomes a blessing. It's not a disability. I thank God for cerebral palsy!"[2] David knows the joy only God's Holy Spirit can give.

THE ESSENTIAL SOURCE OF TRUE JOY

The fountainhead of all joy is the Holy Spirit, and to be filled with the Holy Spirit is to be filled with a joy that is independent of all of life's circumstances. That's why the joy and peace of the Holy Spirit are referred to as a joy and peace which "transcends all understanding" (Phil. 4:7). To unbelievers, it just doesn't make sense when they see people like David filled with joy; there seems to be no reason whatsoever for it.

One of my church members was laughing about confounding a checker and a bag boy at the grocery store. Ruthie is a mature Christian who is filled with the joy of the Holy Spirit, and typically this joy overflows on those with whom she comes into contact. This incident occurred late one afternoon when she made a dash to the grocery store to pick up some items for her dinner preparation. After standing in line for a while with all the after-work crowd, Ruthie finally made it to the checker who looked haggard as she asked, "How ya doin'?"

To which Ruthie replied, "Oh, honey, I am great! I have had a wonderful day! It's kind of you to ask. How's your day been?"

The checker appeared to not know how to respond to the exuberance of her customer.

Finally, she eked out a response, "I'm not used to really getting an answer from folks. If they say anything, it's usually a complaint about having to shop or having to stand in line so long. Why are you so happy?"

Ruthie, who is used to people asking her about her joy, had the checker right where she wanted her! She told her and the bag boy about God's being the Source of her unending joy and that they, too, could know this joy.

The bag boy then carried Ruthie's groceries to her car, a 1956 T-Bird, with the license tag, "GODS GFT."

"Great car! Is it a gift?" he asked.

"No, the car is not a gift. It's salvation that is the gift! It is like I told you and the checker God has the greatest gift of all for each of us," Ruthie explained.

Ruthie's obvious joy and love for the Lord are irrefutable evidence of the presence of the Holy Spirit in her life.

The Bible records times when "inexplicable" joy was exhibited. Once was when Paul and Silas were severely beaten with rods, thrown into a prison, and their feet bound in stocks. It must have been bewildering to the other prisoners to hear them singing and praising God (see Acts 16:22–25). How could they be filled with joy at such a time?

James wrote, "Consider it pure joy, my brothers, whenever you face trials of many kinds" (James 1:2). Peter likewise wrote, "In this you greatly rejoice, though now for a little while you may have had to suffer grief in all kinds of trials" (1 Pet. 1:6). He added that those whose faith was genuine were "filled with an inexpressible and glorious joy" (v. 8).

The presence of the Holy Spirit in Ruthie's life has also brought her inexplicable peace in times of adversity. Ruthie has faced some serious challenges in recent years. Six years ago she was inside her house when it took a direct hit from a tornado. Although her home was damaged, she praised God for His protection of her life. Three years later, while Ruthie was out shopping, her house was gutted by fire. She said her neighbors commented afterward about her calmness as she arrived home to a house engulfed in flames. Ruthie said although shock could have contributed to her calmness, she knows it was a result of knowing and trusting in God's control—even in this bleak situation. She rejoices in the strong witness God has enabled her to show her neighbors through this disaster.

Ruthie's latest challenge has been having to watch her husband, who went through open-heart surgery two years ago, face cancer and its treatment. Through it all, Ruthie says they both have had "peace that passes all understanding."

Throughout the New Testament, joy is always linked with the presence and power of the Holy Spirit. Jesus said He would send a Helper and would leave us with a peace that the world cannot give (see John 14:26–27). In the days that followed the Pentecostal outpouring of the Spirit, the believers—now "turbo charged" with the Holy Spirit—enjoyed fellowship together out of "glad and sincere hearts" (Acts 2:46).

You see, whenever people are filled with the Holy Spirit, they are full of joy. Joy and peace are, as the Bible says, the fruit or the evidence of the presence of the Spirit (see Gal. 5:22). The presence of the Holy Spirit in believers' lives also results in changed perspectives and radically different value systems.

Appreciating the things which are most valuable and keeping the right perspective, two supernatural results of being filled with the Holy Spirit, cause believers to desire the things of God rather than the foolishness of the world. For example, the outpouring of the Spirit caused the first Christians to be a group of people characterized by unity, fellowship, and friendship beyond anything the world had known. It was being filled with the Holy Spirit that caused the first Christians to look beyond themselves and share with all those in need (see Acts 2:45). Likewise, I have seen this same sort of love and fellowship exhibited among believers in churches today.

In our church, I am privileged to witness Spirit-filled Christians giving selflessly of themselves and sharing their resources with others in need. One of our Sunday adult Bible study classes lovingly ministers to one of their member couples who has a critically ill child. The members of this class support this family through prayers, calls, cards, visits, and care-giving. They have become an extended family to this couple. Another adult class has written a card to Jeanette and me every week since I became SBC president—assuring us of their love, prayers, and support. I can see the Holy Spirit at work through the lives of these brothers and sisters in Christ.

Being filled with the Spirit produces radical results in the lives of believers that are beyond the secular world's understanding. The apostles' joy in times of persecution defies rational explanation. "They called the apostles in and had them flogged. Then they ordered them not to speak in the name of Jesus, and let them go. The apostles left the Sanhedrin, rejoicing because they had been counted worthy of suffering disgrace for the Name" (Acts 5:40–41).

Why did they rejoice? They rejoiced because they so highly valued the privilege of suffering for His name. Professing Christians sometimes avow things they don't really understand because they recognize that those are things they should believe. Many need to clarify their understanding of the demands of discipleship and the demonstration of the Holy Spirit's power in the lives of true believers. The kind of sincerity and joy demonstrated by the apostles

150

doesn't come from platitudes, but rather from the filling of the Holy Spirit.

With all that is being said about how to find personal peace and happiness in this present chaotic world, the essential answer is quite simple: it is a New Testament Christianity in which believers are filled with the power and presence of the Holy Spirit. You can go through a lot of mental exercises trying to reproduce the fruit of the Holy Spirit in your life. Traumatic experiences may shock you for a time into a changed perspective of life and values. Time, however, will eventually call you back to a former lifestyle and to former loves. There is only one way of maintaining a clear perspective of what's important and reproducing the qualities you desire, and that is by being filled and controlled by the Holy Spirit. Don't let this point escape you. When you are filled and controlled by God's Spirit, the other dynamics of the Christian life begin to fall into place and inexplicable changes will occur!

THE HOLY SMOKE

A young Methodist pastor gathered all the children at the church altar for the children's sermon one Sunday morning. The message was on the Trinity, so the pastor decided to help the children gain a better understanding of the triune God. He had enlisted the services of the high school science teacher in rigging up a Bunsen burner to provide a visual aid. The pastor explained that the Father, Son, and Holy Ghost were the three Persons of the same one Godhead—of one substance, power, and eternity.

As he tried to explain this he showed them some ice. He put the ice in a clear glass beaker and heated it over the burner. He had them note the change in form of ice to water. He asked if the water was still of the same substance as the ice, and the children said, "Yes." He then heated the water a little longer until it turned to steam. Again he asked if the steam was still the same substance as the ice and the water, and the children said, "Yes." He went on to say the ice was like the Father, the water was like the Son, and the steam was like the Holy Ghost. The three were of the same, one substance even though taking three forms.

The young pastor was feeling pretty good about his explanation and decided to quiz the children. He asked the children who the ice was like and all the children said, "The Father!" He asked who could tell him what the water represented and a boy responded,

"The Son!" The pastor concluded by asking who was like the steam. A precious preschool girl shouted, "God's Holy Smoke!"

This little girl didn't have a good understanding of the third Person of the Trinity—but neither do many of us who have been in church for years and years. The Holy Spirit is often referred to as the "unknown Person" of the Trinity. We all have fathers and, consequently, we can relate to the concept of God as Father. We know what a son is, and we understand to some degree God as the Son. But the *Holy Spirit?* That's a little outside the categories of what we experience in the natural world.

The fact He (not "it") is called the "Holy Ghost" in the King James Version of the Bible doesn't make it any easier. In fact, to a person hearing about Christianity for the first time, that might sound a little scary! It is, perhaps, because we can't use tangible, earthly examples to describe the third Person of the Trinity that there is such controversy and so many misconceptions about the personhood and ministry of the Holy Spirit.

The metaphor used in the Bible to describe the ministry and effect of the Spirit is simply air. To a person in New Testament times, air (or wind) was the most intangible, mysterious thing they experienced in the natural world. Jesus said to Nicodemus, "The wind blows wherever it pleases. You hear its sound, but you cannot tell where it comes from or where it is going. So it is with everyone born of the Spirit" (John 3:8).

The Greek word used here for "wind" and "Spirit" are one and the same. It is the word *pnuema*, which denotes to breathe, to blow—breath, wind, and spirit.

Pnuema is found in Revelation 11:11 where the "breath of life from God entered into" the bodies of the dead in the end times. God breathing His *pnuema* in the end is the same God who, when He created Adam, "breathed into his nostrils the breath of life, and man became a living being" (Gen. 2:7). Christians did not fully become alive until the *pnuema* of God came into them at Pentecost.

A pneumatic jack uses air, which is something you cannot see and cannot feel unless it moves. Air is pumped under pressure into a cylinder. The air pressure in turn moves a piston to lift incredible weights. You might say that when the vessel is filled with the *pneuma* tremendous power flows from that vessel. That's what happens to us when we are filled with God's Holy *Pneuma*.

"God's Holy Smoke!" Maybe that little girl understood more than we thought.

152

SPIRIT-FILLED CHRISTIANS

There was a crippled man who used to sit by the side of the road begging for handouts as people passed by on their way to the temple. One day, not long after the outpouring of the Holy Spirit at Pentecost, Peter and John passed by this man. They didn't have any money, but what they did have proved to be much more valuable. "'In the name of Jesus Christ of Nazareth, walk'" Peter told him (Acts 3:6).

Apparently, everyone knew this beggar because his healing caused quite a stir as he went into the temple leaping for joy and praising God. It also drew a big crowd and gave Peter an excellent opportunity for his second open-air evangelistic meeting. This, of course, infuriated the Jewish religious leaders. Consequently, Peter and John were arrested and brought before the Sadducees to be questioned. They asked, "'By what power or what name did you do this?' Then Peter, *filled with the Holy Spirit,* said to them'" (Acts 4:7–8, italics mine).

The Greek text, the language in which the New Testament was written, literally reads, "Peter, having *just been filled* with the Spirit, said to them" That rendering is printed in the margin of various translations of the Bible, such as the New American Standard Bible. It is significant to understand it as it was literally written. Just before he spoke, Peter was filled with the Holy Spirit.

We are indebted to Luke, the author of Luke and Acts, for the use of the phrase, "filled with the Spirit." Eight out of the nine times this phrase is used in the New Testament, it is found in his writings. Another place where Luke uses this terminology is where he discusses what happens after Peter and John returned from their confrontation with the Sadducees. They had a prayer meeting, and "after they prayed, the place where they were meeting was shaken. And they were all filled with the Holy Spirit and spoke the word of God boldly" (Acts 4:31).

There is one more occasion of the filling of the Holy Spirit I would like to point out. On his first missionary journey, in Cyprus, Paul confronted Elymas, the magician. "Then Saul, who was also called Paul, filled with the Holy Spirit, looked straight at Elymas and said, 'You are a child of the devil and an enemy of everything that is right!'" (Acts 13:9–10).

The point here is obvious. The apostles, namely Peter and John, who were filled with the Holy Spirit at Pentecost, were filled again as they stood to witness to Jesus' power. They were once again filled when they got home and called a prayer meeting. Paul had his sight restored and was filled with the Spirit when Ananias prayed for him (see Acts 9:17). Nevertheless, he was *filled again* when he confronted Elymas in the presence of the Roman Proconsul.

What is this filling of the Holy Spirit? Can we, like the apostles, be filled with the Holy Spirit? How are we filled? There is much controversy and disagreement among Christians about the Holy Spirit and, particularly, the baptism of (or with) the Holy Spirit. Evangelicals say that Christians are baptized in the Holy Spirit when they receive Jesus Christ as their Savior. Some Pentecostals and charismatics say the baptism in the Holy Spirit is a second and subsequent experience. Although it is an important debate, the more pressing question is not *when* we were filled with the Holy Spirit, but rather are we *now* filled with the Holy Spirit?

I have occasionally heard people say something like, "Yes, Brother Jim, I was filled with the Spirit back in '83." Though they may have truly been filled then, sometimes I am tempted to ask, "Do you *think* you've leaked any since then?" My concern is whether they are continually being filled with the Holy Spirit?

I am not talking about the Holy Spirit departing from them, but rather the need to continually have the Holy Spirit in control and fulfilling their lives with His power. The key to abundant life is the repeated filling with the Spirit. When was the last time you prayed for a new and fresh filling of the Holy Spirit? Do you need more of the fruit of the Spirit in your life? More love, joy, peace, or patience—like that known by David and Ruthie? Could it be that you again need to be filled with the Spirit?

There is a passage which is helpful in understanding our continual need to be filled. Paul wrote to the Ephesian church: "Do not get drunk on wine, which leads to debauchery. Instead, *be filled with the Spirit* (Eph. 5:18, italics mine).

John Stott points out four important things about this passage.[3] First of all, it is given as a command in the imperative mood. Our being filled with the Spirit is not like the Sunday buffet line at a Morrison Cafeteria. We don't pick and choose what we like and don't like about the Holy Spirit. We are commanded to be filled with the Spirit! It is a nonnegotiable command for believers.

Second, it is given in the plural form. The filling with the Holy Spirit is not just for the selected few who are "really spiritual." The verb, *to fill*, is plural. In his sermon on the day of Pentecost, Peter said concerning the promise of the Holy Spirit, "The promise is for you and your children and for all who are far off—for all whom

154

the Lord our God will call" (Acts 2:39). In other words, the promise of the Spirit is given for every believer.

Third, this verb is given in the passive voice. The text does not say, "Fill yourself up with the Spirit." We need to be careful not to manufacture in our own emotions what we might believe to be evidences of the filling of the Spirit. The New English Bible reads, "Let the Holy Spirit fill you." How do we let the Holy Spirit fill us? We are filled with the Holy Spirit in the same way we came to accept the gift of salvation, that is, through faith, which demands obedience in response. "So then, just as you received Christ Jesus as Lord, continue to live in him, rooted and built up in him, strengthened in the faith as you were taught, and overflowing with thankfulness" (Col. 2:6–7).

We are to "live as children of light (for the fruit of the light consists in all goodness, righteousness and truth) and find out what pleases the Lord" (Eph. 5:8–10). In short, we, as His children, are to live an obedient lifestyle, desiring to bountifully bear the fruit of the Spirit. It is His desire to let the Holy Spirit fill us. We don't have to beg God for the Holy Spirit. He desires to fill us much more than we desire to be filled. We "allow" Him to fill us by ceasing to grieve or offend the Spirit with our attitudes and actions.

Fourth, it is in the present tense. Literally, it would read: *be being filled with the Spirit,* which means to be filled now with the Holy Spirit. Believers need to be continually filled with the Spirit for the present day, for the next challenge, for this hour, forever.

SPIRIT-SPILLED CHRISTIANS

In our consumer-driven society, people have come to approach the local church, and sometime even God Himself, as consumers. Many "shop around" for a church in the same way they look for a new car. They are interested in the product, the cost, and the service. Much of the church growth recorded in any given city represents people moving around from church to church, and does not signify a net gain for the kingdom. "Why did you pick this church?" is a question I periodically ask those going through our new members' classes.

The answers are fascinating: "The church is a real blessing." "The worship service really ministers to me." "I didn't feel I was getting my needs met at my other church."

The central focus of these answers is self. While this may be natural, this should concern the Christian community. There is a problem when Christians become religion-consumers, *takers* rather than *givers*.

As a believer, the issue is not just how much we are being *filled*, but how much we are being *spilled*. We must not think like consumers. We must relinquish the taker mentality. To be Spirit-spilled means that we are not only filled, but are spilled out as well. It is not a question of "how much" of the Spirit is in us, but how much He flows through us.

It's easy to come, sit, and watch. Church-going, and even Christianity, has for many become too much like a spectator sport. This is a dangerous trend today. There are people who come to First Baptist Church of Orlando with the same mentality as when they go to the O-rena to watch the Orlando Magic play basketball—to be spectators, rather than players. The joy of the Lord, however, doesn't just come from being filled, but from being spilled and being used by the Holy Spirit as His instruments of love.

One of the hardest things for secularly trained people to believe is that there is greater blessing in giving than in receiving. It seems impossible to many that it could be more blessed to serve others than to be served.

Dr. Gary Parker is a successful maxil-facial surgeon. There are certain types of surgery which Dr. Parker has performed more than anyone else in the world; however, he uses his skill to benefit others more than himself.

Along with about four hundred other Youth with a Mission staffers, Dr. Parker and his wife live on the *M/V Anastasis*, the flag ship of the Mercy Ships. They don't have a car, a house, or a thick financial portfolio, but they are rich in many other ways. The earthly wealth Dr. Parker possesses is the treasure of an abundant life in Jesus Christ. His fortune is found in his being Spirit-spilled, in being poured out as he performs surgery while the *Anastasis* is berthed in poor, undeveloped nations.

This is hard for many to comprehend. When Dr. Parker speaks to groups of Western doctors, many find the idea of serving others in this fashion inconceivable. They have great difficulty seeing the gain in using talent and training in this way. I find it tragic when professing Christians have such difficulty.

It is encouraging, however, to see those Christians—like Dr. Parker—who have sold out to Christ, denied themselves, and become committed servants. They have learned in a most convincing way a great Kingdom lesson: *The more you're spilled, the more you're filled.*

This principle is dramatically illustrated in the story of the prophet Elisha and a single-parent mother in financial trouble.

> The wife of a man from the company of the prophets cried out to Elisha, "Your servant my husband is dead, and you know that he revered the LORD. But now his creditor is coming to take my two boys as his slaves." Elisha replied to her, "How can I help you? Tell me, what do you have in your house?" "Your servant has nothing there at all," she said, "except a little oil." Elisha said, "Go around and ask all your neighbors for empty jars. Don't ask for just a few. Then go inside and shut the door behind you and your sons. Pour oil into all the jars, and as each is filled, put it to one side." She left him and afterward shut the door behind her and her sons. They brought the jars to her and she kept pouring. When all the jars were full, she said to her son, "Bring me another one." But he replied, "There is not a jar left." Then the oil stopped flowing. She went and told the man of God, and he said, "Go, sell the oil and pay your debts. You and your sons can live on what is left." (2 Kings 4:1–7)

There are many life applications which can be drawn from this story. The woman's oil continued to multiply and flow as long as she, in faith, continued to pour it into empty vessels. When she stopped pouring, the oil stopped multiplying. When we as Christians pour ourselves into the lives of people who are as empty vessels, the fruit of the Spirit in us will continue to grow and multiply as long as we keep pouring. In other words, the more we are spilled, the more we will be filled. The world is not short of empty vessels. We, as believers, need to be willing to be poured out—as was our Lord and Savior, Jesus Christ.

Two of the most amazing people I know are C. R. and Estelle Smith. C. R. was a successful businessman here in Orlando. He was on the verge of opening his fourth retail store when he and his wife felt compelled to share the blessings God had given them. They weren't satisfied or fulfilled by just being takers. They stepped out in faith and founded Frontline Outreach, an organization that helps disadvantaged young people in Orlando. Their ministry, begun about thirty years ago, has impacted countless numbers of young people and families. Today, the Smiths are still pouring their lives into the lives of others. They will tell you that God has continuously multiplied the oil of joy in their lives as a result.

THE WELL-SPRING OF ABUNDANT LIFE

One of my favorite places in the world is our three-hundred-acre family farm in the rolling hills of Robertson County, Tennessee. Out behind the old two-story home of my grandparents, Will and Ruth, there is a huge, deep hole in the ground. The hole is about thirty to forty feet deep and fifty feet wide at the top. As you climb down into that hole, you can feel the temperature drop. As you navigate carefully to the bottom, you can hear the sound of running water. In the depths of the hole, there is a spring of clear, cool water which has been running longer than anyone can remember. We used to find arrowheads left there by Indians who used to come and drink. Generations of my family have enjoyed the water. You don't even have to pump it; it just flows up and out by itself. It doesn't seem like that spring will ever run dry!

The family drinking hole reminds me of Jesus' words to the Samaritan woman at the well: "Everyone who drinks this water will be thirsty again, but whoever drinks the water I give him will never thirst. Indeed, the water I give him will become in him a spring of water welling up to eternal life'" (John 4:13–14).

The water about which Jesus was talking was much more satisfying than the spring water at the family farm. The water about which He spoke was the Holy Spirit. When we receive Him, then He becomes a well-spring, abundant life that flows up from within us. Because the Giver of life abides in us, as believers, we can be filled from within over and over. Just as the widow's oil continued to multiply as long as she continued to pour, the well of life will continue to fill us from within as we are spilled out into empty vessels.

True joy. Most anyone you ask would enthusiastically respond "Yes!" if asked if they would like to be guaranteed true and lasting joy for life. Most seek temporary happiness, however, instead of permanent joy. They miss the true Source of joy. Their perspective of what joy is, and what or who can provide joy, is distorted. They need to focus on the One who alone is the true Source of joy. They need to experience the joy of the filling of the Holy Spirit.

How can they know this joy? Through the "spilling" of the Holy Spirit, we can show others the true Source of joy. Believers are called to show others the Way. My question then is, Why are there so few joyful Christians? Could it be many tanks are low, running on fumes and need to be refilled? The Holy Spirit is waiting to *fill 'er up!*

CHAPTER ELEVEN

OUR PERSPECTIVE OF PASSION

Most days when I drive about our church campus, I see young athletes from our school in training. Many are passionate in their quest to attain optimum performance through conditioning and practice. They are motivated by different things, some overcoming great obstacles, to be competitive in a given sport. These athletes have bought into the desire to meet or surpass team and personal goals. They are out there running in the heat or in the rain, working out in the weight room or in the pool, practicing on the court or on the field. Though they may tire physically, the best don't often allow themselves to get mentally beaten. These dedicated athletes are in the race for the long haul—until the ribbons go about their necks or the trophies are placed in their hands.

PASSION'S DRIVE

I was fascinated when I first read of a young athlete named Patti Wilson. As a teenager, Patti, an epileptic, told her father she wanted to take up running, but she was afraid of having seizures as she ran. Her father, a morning jogger, assured her they could run together, and he could handle any problem she might face. They began jogging together every day.

After a few weeks, she told her father that her passion was to break the world's long-distance running record for women. The record at that point was eighty miles. A freshman in high school, Patti announced, "I'm going to run from Orange County up to San Francisco" (a distance of 400 miles). At that time she also set other yearly goals. "As a sophomore, I'm going to run to Portland, Oregon" (over 1,500 miles). "As a junior, I'll run to St. Louis" (about 2,000 miles). "As a senior, I'll run to the White House" (more than 3,000 miles away).

Patti never saw herself as being handicapped. Her freshman year she—wearing a T-shirt that read I Love Epileptics—completed her run to San Francisco. Her dad ran every mile at her side. Her mom, a nurse, followed in a motor home behind them, in case anything went wrong.

In her sophomore year, Patti's classmates gave their support. They built a giant poster with the words, Run, Patti, Run! (This has since become her motto and the title of a book she has written.) On her second run, en route to Portland, she fractured a bone in her foot. A doctor told her she had to stop her run or she might permanently damage her foot.

"Doc, you don't understand," she said. "This isn't just a whim of mine; it's a magnificent obsession! I'm not just doing it for me; I'm doing it to break the chains on the brains that limit so many others. Isn't there a way I can keep running?" He gave her one option. He could wrap it in adhesive instead of putting it in a cast. He warned her that it would be incredibly painful, and he told her, "It will blister." She told the doctor to wrap it.

She finished the run to Portland, completing her last mile with the governor of Oregon. The newspaper headlines read, "Super Runner, Patti Wilson Ends Marathon for Epilepsy on Her 17th Birthday."

Two years later, after four months of almost continuous running, from the West Coast to the East Coast, Patti—a senior in high school—arrived in Washington, D.C. As she shook the hand of the president, she told him, "I wanted people to know that epileptics are normal human beings with normal lives."

Because of Patti's noble efforts, by 1993, enough money had been raised to open nineteen multimillion-dollar epileptic centers around the country. Her passion made a difference in her life and in the lives of countless others.[1]

Passion may be defined as "an intense desire or feeling." We can be passionate in the stands as we cheer for our favorite athlete or the home team. Our intense desire is to see them win. We can be passionate about life. There is an intensity we bring to living every day. We can be passionately in love, with strong feelings for that someone special. We can be passionate as we enjoy a musical performance—as evidenced by young people hysterically screaming for their favorite performers.

It's not only kids who are passionate for their favorite performers. I heard the story of an adult couple who planned their whole vacation around the availability of tickets for a hot Broadway play. It took them eight months in advance to secure tickets to a matinee performance.

They traveled to New York on the appropriate weekend. They got to the theater in plenty of time, found their seat—center of the second row of the orchestra section—and sat down. Every seat in the theater was filled except for the seat to the left of the couple. The curtain rose and still no one had filled that seat.

At intermission, the husband turned to a woman on the opposite side of the empty seat and said, "This is amazing! We had to buy our tickets eight months in advance. I wonder how there can be an empty seat."

The woman responded, "Well, that seat belongs to me. It was my husband's seat, but he died."

The man was a little shocked and said, "I am terribly sorry. Didn't you have someone whom you could have invited to come with you?"

She responded sadly, "No. They are all at his funeral!"[2]

This woman must have really had a passion to see the play! Our passion drives us to do unbelievable things—good and bad. Our time and energy are focused on the object of the passion. Often nothing can stop the passion-driven person from satisfying his or her desire.

PASSION'S DETERMINATION

How do we develop a passion for something or someone? How do we muster the intensity of passion? How do we determine what is the best object of our passion? Passion is born in desire. A person feels strongly toward a person or a goal and wants a kind of ownership of the object of passion. Passion, positively directed, can energize a person to great accomplishments. It can give him or her the strength to endure incredible opposition and overcome seemingly insurmountable obstacles. Passion is what puts energy into one's days and real life into the process of living.

Who or what is worthy of our passion? Determining this demands self-control and the ability to prioritize the important matters of life. The highest object of our passion should be God. Yet, how often do you hear believers boast of their passion for God? Passion for God is what drives a believer to know Him intimately and to be used by Him effectively. To attain this highest passion calls for the submission of our hearts' desires to God and our total dependence on God to create in us holy desire.

In the hymn, "Spirit of God, Descend Upon My Heart," the writer calls for God the Holy Spirit to come and take control of the passions of his heart:

> Spirit of God,
> descend upon my heart;
> Wean it from earth,
> through all its pulses move."[3]

This hymn writer understood the inherent dangers of his heart being impulsively stirred by all the wrong passions of this world. He goes on to ask God to give him "one holy passion, filling all [his] frame."

So it was with the Bible character Hezekiah. He was a man of great passion. Hezekiah was twenty-five years old when he became king of Judah. His father, Ahaz, had been a wicked king who had closed the temple, stripped it of its furnishings, set up altars at every street corner in Jerusalem, and built high places to the false gods. King Ahaz was so perverse he even sacrificed his own sons in the fire to false idols. Upon his father's death, Hezekiah ascended the throne.

Hezekiah was a godly young man who understood and assumed his responsibility to correct the horrific wrongs of his father. Hezekiah saw where his father's immense failures had led the nation of Judah. He told the priests, "'Now I intend to make a covenant with the Lord, the God of Israel, so that his fierce anger will turn away from us'" (2 Chron. 29:10). His passion was to turn Judah back to God and have God's blessing once again upon His people.

In society, passion coexists with complacency. It is important to determine which kind of existence you want to live. If, because of complacency or indifference, you choose a passionless life, there are two results of which you can be certain.

The first result will be *a life with no direction*. Such a life will be one characterized by confusion and no true satisfaction. A directionless life is like owning a powerful computer that is not pro-

162

grammed or launching a spacecraft with no chartered destination. Both have great potential, but neither will be realized without a plan. You are truly headed nowhere without direction.

It's much like the poem by Richard Wilbur:

> I read how Quixote in his random ride,
> Came to a crossing once,
> and lest he lose
> The purity of chance, would not decide
> Wither to fare, but wished his
> horse to choose.
> For glory lay where ever he might turn.
> His head was light with pride,
> his horse's shoes
> Were heavy, and he headed
> for the barn.[4]

This poem also reminds me of the second result of living a passionless life. Without passion, yours will be a *life driven by someone else's direction.* There will always be plenty of people who have plans for your life—to sign you up for this, to have you support that, to go there, to be where they need you to be. In fact, anyone or any company who has your telephone number can control a part of your life by eating away at your time like mosquitoes nibbling you to death. You must guard against turning over the driver's seat of your life to others.

It stands to reason all passions are not equally worthy, nor are they all holy. If we are to grow in the likeness of Christ, we should passionately pursue those things that will help us better know and conform to His image. *What made Christ passionate?* should be the question on our hearts and minds as we seek to be like him.

Jesus was driven by a singular holy passion when He said, "'I must be about my Father's business'" (Luke 2:49, KJV). What was His Father's business? "'For the Son of Man came to seek and to save what was lost'" (Luke 19:10). Christ was determined—and triumphant—in not being driven by the false passions of Satan or the Pharisees.

Paul, always passionate in his life's pursuits, upon conversion, was driven to emulate the Savior whose followers he had persecuted. He testified to fellow believers: "But one thing I do: Forgetting what is behind and straining toward what is ahead, I press on toward the goal to win the prize for which God has called me

163

heavenward in Christ Jesus. All of us who are mature should take such a view of things. And if on some point you think differently, that too God will make clear to you" (Phil. 3:13–15).

A changed perspective dramatically refocused his passion—making it worthy of his life's investment and making it holy in the eyes of the Lord. Like Paul, we must be equally passionate as we press on toward our goal of following our Savior as He leads us kingdom-ward.

PASSION'S DEDICATION

How do we dedicate ourselves to pursuing a holy passion? How do we pour our lives into the noblest of all pursuits—to attain eternal life with the Father while helping others do the same? It requires immediate action, decisive obedience.

Hezekiah immediately acted upon his passion. In the first month of his reign, he reopened the temple of the Lord and had the priests consecrate themselves and the temple. They removed all defilement from the temple and made repairs. By the sixteenth day of his first month in office the Levites reported: "'We have purified the entire temple of the LORD, the altar of burnt offerings with all its utensils, and the table for setting out the consecrated bread, with all its articles. We have prepared and consecrated all the articles that King Ahaz removed in his unfaithfulness while he was king. They are now in front of the LORD's altar'" (2 Chron. 29:18–19).

Hezekiah reestablished the service of the temple by assembling the city officials and priests together to worship God and to present sacrifices to God. Following these major reforms in worship practices, Hezekiah sought to reunite the tribes of Israel.

The ten tribes of the Northern Kingdom had been conquered by the Assyrians. Many of these Israelites had been dispersed to other nations; however, there were those Israelites who remained. Hezekiah refused to write off these survivors as renegades or apostates. He viewed them as part of his family of faith. (He even named his own son "Manasseh," the name of the leading northern tribe.) He invited all the covenant people of both kingdoms to come to Jerusalem to celebrate the festivals of Unleavened Bread and Passover at the temple.

Hezekiah's reign is probably best remembered for God's deliverance of Jerusalem from the Assyrians in 701 B.C. The huge force of Assyrians, under Sennacherib, threatened the City of God. Its leaders blasphemed Jehovah God in their taunting of the people of

God. Hezekiah, who had initially paid tribute to Assyria, had learned to put his faith in Almighty God, not in diplomacy. He took a dual approach in protecting Jerusalem. First, he took control of the water supply (to prevent the Assyrians access to the water), fortified the city wall and equipped his army. Secondly, he put his total trust in God and encouraged his people to do likewise. "'Be strong and courageous. Do not be afraid or discouraged because of the king of Assyria and the vast army with his, for there is a greater power with us than with him. With him is only the arm of flesh, but with us is the LORD our God to help us and to fight our battles'" (2 Chron. 32:7–8).

The Bible says the people had confidence in Hezekiah and in God. A great victory was won against the Assyrians, ending their threat against the people of God. Hezekiah's passion to do what was right and good in the eyes of the Lord yielded tremendous accomplishments for his rule as king: reformed worship, a reunited kingdom, and a reign independent of foreign domination. "From then on [Hezekiah] was highly regarded by all the nations" (2 Chron. 32:23).

Misdirected passion, however, can yield havoc. Imagine the power generated by a dam if it were not properly harnessed. There could be great devastation instead of the intended destination of energy under control. So it is with our lives. When God is the Source of our passion and the Controller also, our lives can yield tremendous kingdom power. Like Hezekiah, we must dedicate our lives to God's purpose. We can be most successful in doing so when we earnestly seek God's plan for our lives and passionately dedicate our energy to doing His will through our lives. How can we best know His plan for our lives?

Consider the acrostic: **P** rayerful
A ttainable
S pecific
S trategy
I magination
O riginal
N ow

As we dedicate the passion we have for doing the Lord's will and work in our lives, we must be *prayerful* about seeking the Lord's guidance and control. This is what Hezekiah did when he worshiped and brought sacrifices to God. "Hezekiah trusted in the LORD, the God of Israel" (2 Kings 18:5). The historian also states, "He held fast to the LORD and did not cease to follow him" (v. 6).

165

Sensing and trusting God's leadership, we then set *attainable* goals which we desire to accomplish with His help. Attainable is the key. If I decide that my passion is not to preach but rather sing like Pavarotti, I may need to rethink things. I might possibly be able to sound something like Johnny Cash, but never Pavarotti. This would not be an attainable goal for me. God has enabled me to better handle the spoken word rather than the sung word. As king, Hezekiah was in a unique position to affect great reform for his nation. This reform was attainable for him with God's help.

Once I set attainable goals, I must be *specific* in the ways I am going to attain these goals. If I am certain God has called me to preach, then I should equip myself to do it as well as I possibly can. Seminary is one specific way to attain this goal. I could then seek opportunities to preach or teach. There are specific things I can do to become a preacher. Hezekiah took specific steps to bring about reform. He cleansed the temple, had the priests and the worship articles consecrated, and called for worship and sacrifice.

Next, I need a *strategy* for accomplishing these specific, attainable goals. This involves setting short-term goals which are congruous with long-term, life goals. Having short-term goals helps in keeping my passion from being diminished when it takes many years to accomplish long-term goals. What I am striving for is living well-managed days which consistently reflect a well-managed life.

"This is what Hezekiah did throughout Judah, doing what was good and right and faithful before the LORD his God. In everything that he undertook in the service of God's temple and in obedience to the law and the commands, he sought his God and worked wholeheartedly. And so he prospered" (2 Chron. 31:20–21).

Hezekiah's strategy was to live well-managed days, day in and day out. He steadfastly did what was right and pleasing in the eyes of God. This, too, should be my goal. You may not be able to map out the years, but you *are* able to dedicate each day to serving God with a holy passion. You can do this by taking it hour by hour, task by task, always with life goals in mind.

Strategizing to manage your life doesn't mean to think small. Sometimes in living day in and day out, you may lose your vision of what you might be able to do if you only allowed God to stretch you a little. This is where your God-given *imagination* can be helpful in attaining even greater goals. A great question you should periodically ask yourself is: If I could imagine myself doing

166

anything I wanted to do, what would it be? The answer might help you evaluate if you are truly living your life's passion. If what you imagine differs greatly from what you are presently doing, you may need to reevaluate your attainable goals and your strategy for reaching these goals. Don't dream too small!

God's plan for your life is *original.* The only person you should imitate is Jesus Christ. Otherwise, be the person God has created you to be. Yours should be an original plan fueled by a passion that is uniquely yours. Don't let others put you into a mold. The only image to which you should conform is that of Jesus. Had Hezekiah followed his father's passions, his reign and his life would have been dramatically (and tragically) different. Hezekiah broke Ahaz's mold and became the godly king God intended to rule Judah.

Following Hezekiah's example of not hesitating to follow his godly passion, we must seek to do the same *now.* We should not put off until tomorrow pursuing what God would have us do today. Like Hezekiah, we can immediately enjoy God helping us attain short-term goals. "Hezekiah and all the people rejoiced at what God had brought about for his people, because it was done so quickly" (2 Chron. 29:36). The discipline of deliberately imple menting God's plan for your life should start *now*

PASSION'S DESTINATION

Where's your passion going to take you? If it is a godly passion, it should draw you closer to God. If it is a self-indulgent passion, it will lead you away from God. Following the **p-a-s-s-i-o-n** model, you will see results. Sometimes these results will put you in a position of having to learn how to manage blessings poured out on you by God. Personal success can be hard to manage. It may turn your thoughts away from pleasing God and to indulging your sinful desires.

This is, unfortunately, what happened to Hezekiah. There were definite short-term accomplishments for Hezekiah. The first fourteen years of his kingship were greatly blessed by God. As long as he sought to do God's will in his reign and for Judah, his achievements were amazing. There was security for his nation, enjoyment of worship, great building and the amassment of tremendous personal and national wealth (see 2 Chron. 32:27). Hezekiah, however, began to take pride in "his" achievements. God punished Hezekiah for his false pride by making him deathly ill. When Hezekiah repented and sought God's forgiveness, God miraculously healed him (see 2 Kings 20:1–11; 2 Chron. 32:24–26).

Hezekiah made another serious mistake. Upon receiving a delegation of Babylonian emissaries, he flaunted "all that was in his storehouses—the silver, the gold, the spices, and the fine oil—his armory and everything found among his treasures. There was nothing in his palace or in all his kingdom that Hezekiah did not show them" (2 Kings 20:13). His poor judgment would ultimately bring disaster on Judah.

Hezekiah's long-term goals would not be realized. He had failed to keep the end in mind. Judah would fall (although not during his lifetime) with the Babylonian conquest of Jerusalem. Judah and Israel would not be reunited as a nation. Hezekiah was only fifty-four years old when he died. Despite his failures, "all Judah and the people of Jerusalem honored him when he died" (2 Chron. 32:33). While the greatness of Hezekiah is remembered and honored, think how much more effective he could have been as a king had he persevered in pursuing his holy passion.

We can learn from Hezekiah's accomplishments and failures. In all decisions we should seek God's guidance. If we rely too heavily on our own sufficiency, then ego and pride can smother the holy passion that should be ablaze in us. We, too, need to keep the end in mind.

My dad died recently. During the latter stages of his illness, my mom, my brother, and I went to the cemetery to choose burial sites. We decided to buy a family plot with lots for my parents, for my brother and myself, for our spouses, and for our children—should they choose to be buried there. We also had to pick out a Henry family marker. We wanted that marker, not only to carry the family name, but also to bear witness to Christ long after we are gone. My mom and my brother gave me the responsibility of deciding what we would have etched on the stone. I prayed about it and thought about it for a good while. I finally decided on John 6:40: "'For my Father's will is that everyone who looks to the Son and believes in him shall have eternal life, and I will raise him up at the last day.'" That verse captured for me the essence of the faith embraced by our family and what I wanted those who passed by the marker to know was important to our family.

Some months ago, I received a note that began with the saying: "You are not ready to live your life until you know what you want written on your tombstone." For our family, we wanted our tombstone to reflect the lives we have chosen to live. Our desire has been to live lives that positively reflect, and direct others to, our Savior. In the end, what do you want to have written on your tombstone? What is your perspective of where you want your passions to take you—to the heavenly throne of grace or the judgment seat of disgrace? Is it your greatest desire to hear the Lord's words, "'Well done, good and faithful servant!'" (Matt. 25:21)?

CHAPTER TWELVE

OUR PERSPECTIVE OF DREAMS

Have you ever experienced bitter disappointment? Have you ever had hope crushed? Have you ever poured your time, energy, money, or self into a project and had it come to the edge of reality only to see it shoved over the edge by circumstances or individuals and left dashed on the rocks of shattered dreams? Have you ever felt let down or deserted by God on something you really felt like He was in, yet for no discernible reason, He seemed to pull the plug on your dream? If so, join the crowd of humanity that has shared similar disappointment, loss, grief, and pain.

HOLD ON TO YOUR DREAMS

Each of us can identify with disappointment—from the smallest child, whose expectations were not met by parents, to the oldest adult, forgotten by family members who are too busy to care. A few years ago, a woman wrote to Ann Landers about the greatest disappointment of her life. In her letter, she described the dream her well-meaning dad had spoiled.

> During World War II, I lived in Los Angeles. It was an exciting place to be. Thousands of soldiers, sailors and Marines were here waiting to be shipped to the South Pacific.

I was 19, and "Bud," my high school sweetheart, was already overseas. We weren't engaged, but we wrote to one another three or four times a week. Then one night at the Hollywood Palladium, I met Ken Morrison, a handsome Marine. It was magic. We danced for hours and talked all night. Ken was the man I had dreamed of all my life. We were together every possible minute for three glorious weeks before he was shipped out.

I will never forget his teary-eyed smile when he promised to write. We knew we belonged together and prayed that one day it would be possible.

I was living with my dad at the time (my mom was dead), and I worked as a secretary. Several weeks went by, and I asked my dad every evening, "Any mail for me?" There were plenty of letters from Bud but none from Ken.

Every time I read about some awful battle involving Marines, my heart sank. After six months and no words from Ken, I was certain he had been killed. Bud came home in 1946, and we were married. We had three children. I knew that I had settled for a dull, but stable, existence. I never stopped mourning for Ken. He was the true love of my life.

When dad died in 1958, I went to his house to sort out his belongings. In the attic was an old trunk. As I was digging through his papers and personal effects, I ran across a bundle of letters addressed to me. There were dozens of letters held together by leather bands. When I discovered they were from Ken, I thought my heart would break. Then I heard my children's voices in the next room, and I knew I had to throw those letters away, unopened. It took all the strength I could muster, but I did it.

When my oldest child was 18, I divorced Bud. By that time my marriage had become so sterile and lifeless, I couldn't bear it. I remarried in 1970. It was a poor choice and we divorced in 1985. Now I occupy myself with volunteer work at the hospital and a few classes at the community college.

I am lonely and very sad when I think of what my life would have been. I often daydream about Ken and hope that he found a wonderful girl, is happily married and, like me, has grandchildren to love. But I can't help wondering whether he ever thinks about me.[1]

171

Life is tough. You, to one degree or another, are going to have to deal with disappointment. You may have been in a situation in which you were so greatly disappointed from that time on it shaped your perspective of yourself and your relationships with others. Disappointment may have altered the course of your life. Perhaps the pain of disappointment is not in the past. You may presently be facing a situation which has you on the verge of losing, or even walking away from, the most valuable things in your life. Circumstances have left you disappointed, disillusioned, and bitter. Don't lose hope. God has provided a way to deal with even the greatest disappointments in life. Don't give up! Hold on to your dreams.

DREAMS THAT MOTIVATE YOU

What dreams are most vivid in your mind right now? I am not speaking of the kind of dreams you have when you are sleeping. I am talking about the kind you dream when you are wide awake. These dreams get you out of bed and going in the morning? What are your dreams?

HANNAH'S DREAM

Hannah had a dream. She was a remarkable person. She was a nineties kind of woman, even though she lived during the period of the judges in Old Testament times. She was motivated by dreams of what she wanted in life and refused to be held back by societal norms as she pursued them. She was not afraid to take risks to achieve what she saw as her God-given role in life. She was a gentle, yet passionate dreamer.

Hannah, like many women today, had a difficult marriage. She faithfully stayed in the marriage and desired to make it work. Her marital problems were definitely not the run-of-the-mill present-day problems, as her husband, Elkanah, was a polygamist. He had two wives: Hannah and Peninnah, her nemesis.

Polygamy was practiced, to some extent, among the Israelites of that era. This practice seemed to provide the husband greater assurance he would have sons—to keep his name alive and to help support the family. Polygamy, while an ancient Near Eastern custom, was not God's plan. God would have preferred Elkanah's putting his trust in Him, rather than multiple wives, to provide male heirs.

172

Hannah's marital problems were compounded by the plight of her not being able to have children. Today, many couples decide to put off having children until careers are established—or to not have children all together. In a male-centered society, a woman's not having children—more specifically, not having a son—was to fail her husband. It was also perceived as a curse from God.

Hannah's dream was to give her husband a son. Her dream was to be loved and appreciated by Elkanah in the same way as he loved his other wife, Peninnah. Her dream was to know God's blessing and provision in her life. Her dream was to serve God as a godly and devoted mother. Her dream was her life's passion.

PASSION'S DREAM

As a believer, where will your godly passion take you? Not very far, if you don't dream. About what kind of dream am I writing? I am focusing on God-given dreams which lead to God-given results.[2] These dreams are goals, desires, or plans God gives an individual for that person to be all God has designed that person to be and for that person to do the life's work God has designed that person to do.

As one enters the grounds of First Baptist Church, Orlando, there is a huge rock at the fork in the road. One of the men of our church found this eleven-ton rock near Gainesville, Florida. He had it loaded on a flatbed truck, brought to the church, and placed in its strategic location to serve as a reminder of our church's dream.

A few years prior to that rock's placement, our church had voted to relocate to the present site. When we were planning our relocation, we knew it would take an initial expenditure of several million dollars. We brought in experts who studied our church, our patterns of giving, demographics, and the average incomes of members and prospective members. These experts projected the maximum amount our people could possibly give over a three-year period was $10 million. This was an extremely optimistic goal.

Our church had an all-night prayer meeting. As time was drawing close to the commitment day of our financial campaign, we prayed God would move in the hearts of our people. We prayed He would lead His church in this time of financial commitment.

During the course of that evening's prayer meeting, one of our men stood up and asked the question, "How much money do we

173

need to really get us off to a good start at the new property?" I responded by telling him the architects and contractors believed we needed $12 million, though the long-term project would cost a great deal more. This man responded by asking, "If we have enough faith to ask God for $10 million, why don't we ask Him for $12 million instead?"

God used his words to stir our people's hearts. The congregation decided unanimously to change the goal to $12 million. We had already printed brochures with $10 million typed on them. We had to go back, strike out the ten, and replace it with a twelve. We printed on these brochures the new words, "God's Goal."

We had a great initial dream. Yet God gave us the courage and the faith to dream even bigger dreams. By His gracious provision, He allowed us to reach our new goal some weeks later. To this day, we continue to pursue God's dream, His vision, for our church. The huge rock at our church's entrance serves as a constant reminder of the theme of that first campaign, "Upon This Rock," and of our need as His body to keep dreaming His dreams.

DISAPPOINTMENTS THAT MOLD US

TESTING OF A DREAM

How do you know if your dream is God's dream? How do you know if it conforms to His perfect will for your life? How do you know if your dream will move your life ahead in the direction God has charted for your life's course? How do you know if your dream is worthy of your life's calling?

It has been said that none of us are really adequate dreamers.[3] If this is true, how then do we check the adequacy of our dreams? Paul, the apostle, says we have a personal responsibility to present ourselves to God "as living sacrifices, holy and pleasing to God." We are not to "conform any longer to the pattern of this world, but be transformed by the renewing of" our minds. Then we "will be able to test and approve what God's will is—his good, pleasing, and perfect will" (Rom. 12:1–2).

We, as Christians, need to learn to dream with our eyes open. Our eyes should not only be opened, but focused on Jesus Christ. We need to be wide awake to the things of God and obediently offer ourselves as His servants ready to rouse a sleepy world. We should not buy into the world's dreams but seek to possess His dreams. We must submit to His dream instruction, which sometimes includes the course "Testing 101!"

I can remember a time in my life when it seemed God was making me repeat the "testing course" over and over. Perhaps, I didn't make a good enough grade the first ten or twelve times I took the course; He thought I needed a refresher course. Or, it could have been He liked my final performance so well, He moved me up to a higher level course! Whatever His reason, I was back in class again—this time during a period of adjustment of the direction and philosophy for "doing church" in a more biblical way at First Baptist, Orlando.

Change never comes easily, and this was certainly no exception. The process of retooling our church took several years, endless meetings, defections of members we loved, anonymous hate letters, twisted rumors, and a wide range of disappointments, doubts, and difficulties.

In retrospect, I see it as a time which drove me to my knees in prayer, to the Bible for assurance that we were in obedience to God, and to trusted friends for counsel and encouragement. Out of it, I believe, I grew in wisdom and patience. I learned to trust in the ability of God to bring His will to bear upon individuals and groups, which I saw worked out in such a way that I am still astounded by its scope and thoroughness. While testing like this is stressful and often painful, I have come to appreciate what God can accomplish through the process.

Hannah was tested. It seems as though her barrenness and marriage woes should have been testing enough, but God required more. Did her dream need testing? No, it wasn't her dream which needed testing. Hers was a good dream. It was a dream given by God. In fact, it was an important first part of a much bigger dream: the uniting of Israel under a king. It was Hannah, instead, who needed testing. God needed to prepare her to realize her dream come true.

How was she further tested? Her rival-as-wife, Peninnah, taunted her relentlessly. The Bible records that Peninnah provoked Hannah "in order to irritate her. This went on year after year" (1 Sam. 1:6–7). It is easy to understand what was happening here. If Peninnah kept Hannah upset all the time, how could Hannah be as attractive and as loving a mate as she would have been without all this stress? Not possible. Peninnah was smart, and she definitely was playing for keeps.

175

Hannah was further upset each time she went to the temple at Shiloh. There, in the midst of families going to offer their worship and their sacrifices, she felt all alone without a child. Again, at these times "her rival provoked her till she wept and would not eat" (v. 7). When his two wives were at each others' throats, Elkanah would try to smooth things over by asking, "'Hannah, why are you weeping? Why don't you eat? Why are you down-hearted? Don't I mean more to you than ten sons?'" (v. 8).

The Bible does not say Hannah received any comfort or reassurance from her husband's questioning. It appears this guy was clueless as to her real needs. A somewhat typical male response is found in the last part of verse 8 when Elkanah focuses the attention on himself. If he can't comfort her, then he might as well seek some loving reassurance from her! What she needed and longed to hear from him was that *she* meant more to *him* than ten sons. Her husband remained a part of Hannah's testing.

When she had no one who could understand her needs or her dream, then "in bitterness of soul Hannah wept much and prayed to the LORD" (v. 10). As this woman poured out her soul to the Lord, Eli, the priest, observed her and accused her of being drunk (see vv. 13–14). Hannah couldn't win! God was using everyone in this woman's life to test her. (Clue: Her dream must have been awfully significant to require this degree of dreamer-testing.)

Why are we, as dreamers, tested? Doug Murren has suggested two important reasons.[4] First, we are tested so our character will match our dreams. Christian character is "a work in progress" for us, as believers. When God gives us a dream, we may need a lot of work on and in our lives to enable us to handle the dream. True, God the Holy Spirit can enable us to do all things. What do you think testing is? It's one of His enabling tools to equip us to handle the challenges of our dreams.

That's what happened with Joseph in the Bible (Gen. 37, 39–45). God gave him incredible dreams, and then he was put through some of the most intensive testing imaginable. Joseph's character and devotion to God were targeted. Why? He had to be tested to be equipped to handle the magnitude of the dream God gave him.

This leads to a second reason we are tested. God's dreams are bigger than we are. Another truth is, God's tests can be bigger than we are. Why? Both cases cause us to depend on Him. Our sufficiency and strength should always be in God—and God alone. As with Hannah, it usually is a pretty good clue that the test or the dream is from God when things don't work out easily. The greater the dream, the greater the testing.

DISAPPOINTMENT AS GOD'S APPOINTMENT

A disappointment is an act or a feeling of not having expectations, hopes, or dreams fulfilled. A disappointment occurs not as appointed or planned. We may be disappointed by circumstances, by other people, or in ourselves. How we respond to disappointment when our dreams are tested influences our lives and our relationship to God.

Circumstances which lead to disappointment may well be beyond our control. For instance, the faithful employee who dreams of advancement is passed over for a well-deserved promotion. The decision-making was not in the control of the employee, but rather in the hands of corporate executives more concerned with bottom-line numbers than fairness among the ranks. A performer may not initially get the breaks needed to get professionally established as an entertainer. Disappointment comes time and time again as he is rejected after numerous auditions. The sweet eleventh grader who does not get an invitation from her dream guy to the junior-senior prom is tested by circumstances which may be beyond her control.

Disappointments come—often at the hands of others. Such was the case with Tom, a successful young businessman who was very active in the church. His marriage seemed solid and happy, until, out of the blue, his wife of several years informed him that she no longer loved him and wanted a divorce. His dream of sharing a life and a family with the woman he loved seemed shattered.

Tom, however, refused to give up on his marriage. He and his wife came to see me for counseling. He told her how much he loved her and how he believed they could make their marriage work. I'll never forget her response to him. She stared at him with some of the steeliest eyes and one of the hardest looks I have ever seen, and coldly responded that she didn't love him. In fact, she said she didn't even like him and didn't want to be near him or see him anymore. I cringed as I listened to her expel her venom on this man who dearly loved her. The wife gave no other reasons for wanting to leave the marriage, except she was ready for a change. She had grown tired of her husband. Tom's disappointment in his wife was tremendous. Divorce was imminent.

177

We can also be disappointed in ourselves. When the testing of a dream comes, we may blame ourselves. We may feel we are not worthy to possess lofty dreams. We fail to figure in the "God Factor": God **x** Dreamers **=** Infinite Dreams Realized. We think too small. We limit the pursuit of dreams to our singular pursuit, failing to accept God in what should be a joint venture.

Someone has said our disappointments are God's appointments to accomplish His perfect will in us.[5] Believing this to be true offers peace of mind even when we find it hard or impossible to make any rhyme or reason out of disappointments in our lives. God has His reasons for allowing us to be tested and disappointed in our pursuit of dreams.

We must not fail to recognize God's sovereignty. He is *always* in control—even when it appears to us everything is out of (our) control. God is not controlled by circumstances or individuals. As He gives the dreams, He, too, gives the testing and allows disappointment.

The 121st Psalm frames beautifully the sovereign control of God.

> I lift up my eyes to the hills—
>   where does my help come from?
>
> My help comes from the LORD,
>   the Maker of heaven and earth.
>
> He will not let your foot slip—
>   he who watches over you will not slumber;
>
> indeed, he who watches over Israel
>   will neither slumber nor sleep.
>
> The LORD watches over you—
>   the LORD is your shade at your right hand;
>
> the sun will not harm you by day,
>   nor the moon by night.
>
> The LORD will keep you from all harm—
>   he will watch over your life;
>
> the LORD will watch over your coming and going
>   both now and forevermore.

God has a plan for each of His children. All details are ordered according to His perfect will. We face disappointment when we attempt to set up our own plan. When things don't happen according to our plan and our dream begins to crumble, we may feel disappointed or even defeated. The problem is we have substituted our plan for God's plan! His plan is best. His plan is sovereign.

God was in sovereign control of Tom's marriage. Tom would not give up hope for his marriage. He kept praying, kept believing, kept pursuing a way to heal the situation. He asked God to save their marriage. Then, as if this man had not been through enough, Tom was in a terrible automobile accident. As he lay in the hospital, fighting for his life, something incredible happened. His wife came to him and said she did not want to lose him. She said she realized how much she and their children needed him. She wanted him well and back in her life.

The accident occurred several days before their divorce was to be finalized. His wife withdrew the divorce papers. She stayed by his side as he regained his health. The love she thought she had lost was rekindled.

Some time later, I saw the two of them and asked how things were going. They said it was like they were on their honeymoon—but one much better than their first. All the disappointment and hurt was behind them. Their marriage was much stronger and healthier—and under God's control. Tom's impossible dream, which was rigorously tested, found fulfillment in God's superior plan for his life and his marriage. It was all better than Tom ever dreamed.

DETERMINATION THAT MEASURES YOU

HANNAH'S GROWTH

Hannah initially responded to the testing of her dream through tears of disappointment and bitterness. She was miserable, depressed and unable to eat. She expressed her deep troubles in terms of "great anguish and grief" (1 Sam. 1:16). After her misery persisted for years, a change became evident in her life. Through testing, Hannah grew in her reliance on God. It was to Him she began to pour out her soul. She grew in her trust of His sovereign control. She grew in her understanding of her role in the dream. She determined to have confidence in the faith she professed.

Hannah came to the temple at Shiloh and "made a vow, saying, 'O LORD Almighty, if you will only look upon your servant's misery and remember me, and not forget your servant but give her a son, then I will give him to the LORD for all the days of his life'" (v. 11). Hannah realized God's dream for her life required her relinquishing her son to God. While Hannah was crying for a son, the nation of Israel was crying for a king. If God was going to use her son as a king-maker, He first had to have total control over the boy's life—and the mother's dream. Hannah made a solemn vow to God in submission to His sovereign plan for her life—and the life of her son, should God so bless her.

Hannah grew leaps and bounds in her faith. Her demeanor changed immediately upon Eli's confirmation of the Lord's blessing on her life. Hannah "went her way and ate something, and her face was no longer downcast" (v. 18). She was responsive to her husband (see v. 19) and patiently waited on the Lord to determine the outcome (see v. 20). Her words were no longer bitter expressions of disappointment and doubt, but were jubilant expressions of praise for what the Lord had accomplished through her (see 1 Sam. 2:1–10).

DREAMER'S GROWTH

As dreamers, we can find in Hannah a model for our faith. Yes, we, too, can be severely disappointed by dreams which go unfulfilled and by God's testing of us. We, too, can cry out in bitterness of soul. Like Hannah, if our testing draws us closer to knowing God and relying on God, we will have every reason to praise God.

Like Hannah, if we believe our dream is of God and properly reflects God's will for our life, we must be persistent in our determination to see our dream fulfilled. It has been said perseverance is not a long race; it is many short races, one after another.[6] The training of marathon runners consists of many shorter runs to build up endurance for the long run.

So it is with life. We have to learn to pass the pop quizzes before we can handle the mastery tests of life. There are important lessons for us to learn before we can graduate to realizing our dream. We must be determined to make the grade in our divine schooling by the Master. (Praise God, He gives us a tutor in the Holy Spirit!)

From Hannah we can learn to *petition* God for our needs. When we look anywhere other than to our heavenly Father, we will face disappointment. Other people will sooner or later let us down. Answers to the tough tests we face can only come from God. He is the Source of every need and the Fulfiller of every dream. We must come to Him in prayer, asking Him to help us relinquish control of our lives, and rely on Him.

At times, we may need to pour out our souls to the Lord as Hannah did. We may even face the need to make a solemn vow to God. Like Hannah, we desperately need to turn to Him unless we're willing to settle for less than His best dream for our lives.

Again, our *perspective* must be addressed. Are we going to be so embittered by disappointment that we lose all hope of our dream coming true? Are we going to give up under the weight of testing? Hannah's perspective kept her dream alive. Though her anguish was often great, she never lost hope in what God could accomplish through her. When society would have questioned her persistence with this dream and doubted her devotion to God, her perspective allowed her to see things differently. She saw an unorthodox solution, as evidenced by her vow, to achieving her life's dream. Her perspective allowed her to dream big!

GOD'S MEASURE

We can learn some important lessons about determination and "dreaming big" from the world of business. Two brothers, Dick and Maurice, were running a drive-in restaurant in the desert heat of San Bernardino, California. The restaurant had a lengthy menu and a lot of wasted food. They had a dream of cutting the drive-in service and changing to a low-priced, assembly line place serving only burgers, fries, and drinks. They followed their dream and made the changes in their restaurant.

Everybody hated it. They no longer employed snazzy carhops. The customers stood in lines to get their food orders. People began complaining about having to wait on themselves and having to throw away their own trash. The changes had turned their little eatery into a "complete disaster," according to Dick. The two brothers considered giving up on their dream.

The turnaround came when the two brothers—Dick and Maurice McDonald—added a third partner named Ray Kroc. Ray brought fresh, innovative ideas into the partnership. McDonald's golden arches serve as a visual reminder of the dream these men shared. Their tested dream changed fast-food and restaurant history.[7]

I love the quote, "Great dreams of great dreamers are never fulfilled; they are always transcended."[8] Hannah's dream was a great dream, but God transcended her dream with one which was even

181

greater. Hannah's prayers were answered. She and Elkanah gave birth to Samuel, whose name meant "heard of God." She did not forget her vow. Because her testing had made her strong, she was able to give the child she dearly loved to the Lord who needed this child more than she.

God had a plan in which Samuel was pivotal. He was to be Israel's last judge. He was to be the one God used in the selection and the anointing of Saul, and then David, as king. There was no way Hannah could have known the proportions of her dream. It was big! She had to grow into it.

God did not forget her. He gave her and Elkanah five other children—three sons and two daughters. It is not hard for us to deduce that Hannah must have experienced love—of her husband and of her children—to a depth she had not previously known. She must have likewise enjoyed the peace and satisfaction that comes from having an important dream realized. Can you imagine what she must have felt as she saw her son grow into a king-maker? God's measure of goodness and blessing must have been experienced by Hannah to depths few have ever known.

As God transformed Hannah through her testing, He, too, seeks to transform us into mature Christians who are determined to know and to handle His dreams for our lives. God desires our knowing the full measure of His grace and love as offered through Jesus Christ. We can know this, at least in part, while we are still on this earth. Dreams are one means given to us by God as a fore-taste of what God will ultimately do for us in heaven. If we allow God to change our perspective, from seeing dream-testing as cursed punishment to viewing it as blessed tutelage, we can enjoy the benefits of His teaching us how to dream big. Go ahead, dream the dreams which can only be dreamed and realized by the children of the King of kings!

CHAPTER THIRTEEN

OUR PERSPECTIVE OF ETERNITY

Several years ago, I was traveling by car in the state of Alabama. As I topped a hill, I came upon a terrible car accident which had occurred only minutes before. There was wreckage everywhere, and smoke was billowing from one of the cars. Being among the first on the scene, I stopped my car to see if I could be of assistance. I saw a man lying in a pool of blood in a ditch. I scrambled down the embankment to his aid. As I cradled his head in my arms, his blood covering my clothing, I shouted to him, seeking a response. None came. I continued to try to get a response, to revive him, but he was already dead.

It struck me that only moments before, the lifeless face into which I was looking was full of expression. I am sure he had no idea, prior to the accident, he was living in the last minutes of his life. I stood there dazed as they carried his body away to the morgue. It's hard to describe the wave of emotions which came over me in those traumatic moments.

After the ambulance had gone, I got back in my car and drove down the road to the nearest service station. I went into the restroom to clean up and to change clothes. As I tried to wash off the man's blood, I was still trembling. All kinds of thoughts raced through my mind. He was probably on his way home from work, expecting to have supper with his family when, in one horrifying moment, his life on earth was over.

After I got back in the car, I couldn't help but think about staring at his lifeless body—staring into the face of death. I had thoughts of my own mortality. *If I were suddenly killed in an accident, what would I leave undone? How well-prepared was I to unexpectedly face death?*

WAKE-UP CALLS

Death is scary. Most of us don't like to think about it or talk about it; yet, there is no factor more important in shaping our perspective and our priorities. Nevertheless, most of us just go about our business, knowing life is short but acting as if we will live forever.

Every now and then, we get a wake-up call to reality. Friends die. Family members face death. We attend funerals of loved ones. While we have concern for the grieving and feelings for the departed, our thoughts often return to thoughts about our own mortality. The car accident was a wake-up call for me. It made me reconsider my priorities and my purpose in life. Many others have similar, or more traumatic, wake-up calls.

Unfortunately, instead of waking up, many of us only hit the snooze button and go back to sleep again! If we hit the snooze button too many times, though, we may not wake up in time to seize the opportunity God has given us to sharpen our perspective on death or realize the abundant life we have in Jesus Christ.

I have officiated at numerous funerals in my ministry. No matter how many I conduct, I always seem to walk away with a renewed awareness of life's transience. Funerals are great perspective-shapers. If there is anything which should influence the way I look at life and the way I live my life, it should be the shortness of my time on earth compared to the vastness of eternity. The Bible says, "What is your life? You are a mist that appears for a little while and then vanishes" (James 4:14). A mist may be seen or felt for an instant, but then it is gone and quickly forgotten. That is my life—and yours.

The good we do or the impact we have on humanity must reach to the other side of eternity if it is to be of more than fleeting significance. The urgent and the materially rewarding matters often push aside what eternally matters. Eternity fades so far into the background of our thinking it often has no measurable effect on how we live our lives. The dulling influence of this present world causes us to hit the snooze alarm and puts us back to sleep.

About a year ago on a Saturday afternoon, I was sitting at home watching a football game when the broadcast was interrupted by a special report. Prime Minister Yitzhak Rabin had been shot. The first report indicated he had survived the assassination attempt. A later report confirmed his death. I was saddened by the news.

I have a great love for Israel and her people. The previous year I, as part of the United States delegation attending the official signing of the peace treaty between Jordan and Israel, met Prime Minister Rabin. I found him to be pleasant and polite, very business-like. It was apparent to all that he was excited about the signing of the treaty.

The evening I learned of his assassination I went to bed with a sense of loss and grief, similar to the way I felt when I learned of President Kennedy's assassination. Shortly after midnight, I was abruptly awakened by a phone call from the White House. A group of political and religious leaders were going to Israel to attend Rabin's funeral with the president. Air Force Two would be departing from Andrews Air Force Base at 11:00 A.M. Sunday morning. I was asked to accompany the group. Talk about a wake-up call!

After frantically making some arrangements with my church staff, I was on my way to Washington. By 9:00 A.M. on Monday the group landed in Israel, and we were on our way to the King David Hotel. The experience was overwhelming. It seemed as though there was a soldier with an automatic weapon on every other square meter of the city. (Fifteen thousand soldiers had been stationed in the city of Jerusalem to provide the highest security possible.)

We had only forty-five minutes at the hotel to change clothes before our departure for the funeral. My luggage was inadvertently left on the plane. (Even flying Air Force Two is no guarantee your luggage will arrive at your destination the same time as you!) Because I had dressed casually for the overseas flight, I was not in proper funeral attire. I borrowed a shirt from a lawyer, whom I had gotten to know on the previous trip to Israel and a tie from one of the presidential aides to wear with my sport coat. I was the only person among all the national delegations wearing a casual sport coat! (God certainly has a way of keeping pride in check, doesn't He?)

After a brief stop at the Knesset to view Rabin's body lying in state, we were shuttled by bus to the funeral. As we passed by the hundreds of thousands of people lining the route, it was easy to see the anguish and the anger on their faces. It was as if the entire nation turned out to mourn.

This funeral service began like none other I had ever attended—with the blasting of sirens. It is customary for the city sirens of Jerusalem to sound for one minute a year as a memorial to the Holocaust. This time the sirens sounded for two minutes as a memorial to this respected leader. First, a single air raid siren began blaring. Then, one after another, all the sirens throughout the city began to sound. It sounded like the city itself was crying.

At the grave site, I was fascinated by the impact of this man's assassination on so many world leaders. I saw assembled there Great Britain's Prince Charles; British Prime Minister John Major; German Chancellor Helmut Kohl; the Queen of Holland; the President of Russia; the Secretary General of the United Nations; the President of the United States, Bill Clinton; the Speaker of the House of Representatives, Newt Gingrich; the Majority Leader of the Senate, Bob Dole; former President George Bush; and former President Jimmy Carter. These powerful leaders and other heads of state laid aside their political ideologies and demanding schedules to pay honor to a fellow leader. They were visibly moved by the tragic event. They were drawn together by death.

After most had left the grave site, Senator Ted Kennedy knelt at Rabin's grave. He had removed a bag of dirt from his brother's grave in Arlington National Cemetery and then mixed it with the dirt of Rabin's grave. This poignant gesture was his way of identifying with Rabin's family's suffering.

It is true that death is the great equalizer. For example, all of these distinguished world leaders at Rabin's funeral were forced, by death, to examine the insecurity and danger associated with their own positions—and more significantly, forced to consider their own mortality. Death accomplished more than any world summit could have in focusing their attention and agendas on this single common issue. Death impacts the perspective of all people—humble or great—at least, for a season.

LIVING ON BORROWED TIME

Pastoring a large congregation, I often come into contact with members who have received news they are facing terminal illnesses. It is never easy to see people, about whom I care, agonizing as they come to grips with suffering and death. It is often encouraging, however, to watch mature Christians in this process. I am touched and blessed by devout believers whose days are numbered by a terminal illness, joyfully anticipating an eternity in heaven. They are supernaturally comforted in their struggles by their trust in God's sovereign control of their lives and God's deep, abiding love for them as His adopted children. They are determined to "die in the faith," even though their pain-ridden bodies might cause others of less faith to question or even curse God. I marvel at the Spirit of God as He equips these saints to deal with life's brevity.

Tom Gurney was such a believer who faced death confidently in the strength of the Lord. He was a respected and distinguished lawyer, the chairman of the Florida Board of Regents, and an active member of our church. He was a great friend—of mine and of the Lord. Tom had enjoyed a long and full life. The time came when he faced death.

I went to see Tom near the end of his life. We reminisced about all the things God had done for us in our lives and recounted many of God's great blessings. I knew it was the last time I would see my friend on this side of eternity. Those were special moments together. We enjoyed a time of prayer. After we prayed, I asked Tom if there was something he would like me to say to all of his friends after he was gone. This man, whose wisdom and advice had been sought by so many people, lifted both hands and said, "Yes, indeed. Tell them to worship the Lord!"

Death had shaped his perspective—but many years before he himself actually faced it. He had an astute understanding of how a believer should live his life under the influence of eternity.

My great-grandmother Pope was also like that. She loved God, and, as a devout Christian, she was always full of thanksgiving for what God had done for her. Even though she suffered greatly as she faced the final stages of cancer, she seldom complained. She continued to praise God in all things.

My most vivid memory of her was my last visit with her. Just a child, I was only slightly taller than the edge of her bed, and I had to stand on tip-toes to look into her eyes as she lay there. I remember her smiling lovingly at me and asking me to recite the Twenty-third Psalm to her. Her face was radiant, even in her weakened condition, as I quoted that beautiful and reassuring passage. Great-grandmother Pope's faith was as focused in death as it was throughout her life.

How can we gain the perspective death gives? How can we appreciate that which is eternal more greatly than that which is temporal? How can we face our own fragile mortality with confidence and assurance of hope beyond death?

ONE MORE YEAR

What if you were told you had a terminal illness and your life expectancy was only one more year at the most? Would you be prepared to face death? How would you live those remaining days in the light of this diagnosis? How would your perspective change?

"The LORD says. . . . 'This very year you are going to die'" (Jer. 28:16). A diagnosis from a doctor is one thing. You can always seek a second opinion. What if your diagnosis was directly from God? How could you refute that kind of prognosis? The Scripture quoted was the Word of the Lord spoken to Hananiah by the prophet, Jeremiah. Talk about a wake-up call!

Hananiah was a man who had fooled many people into thinking he was a man of God. He convincingly spoke the believers' language. He even went as far as to claim he was a prophet, as his father had been a prophet. He said he spoke with the authority of God, yet he only spoke false prophecy. He faced off against Jeremiah. They debated the return of the exiles in Babylonian captivity.

Hananiah said God had revealed to him that the exiles would return to Israel within two years. Jeremiah prophesied their return in seventy years. Both prophets could not be speaking the truth with God's authority. Jeremiah called for a showdown. He told Hananiah God would settle the issue, and God did. The true prophet of God, Jeremiah, delivered God's verdict to Hananiah. He warned Hananiah that he, as a false prophet, had received the Lord's judgment and he would die within the year as penalty.

The Bible doesn't tell us Hananiah's reaction to the prophecy of his death. Did he change his tune? Did he live his life differently from that fateful moment on? Did he come to worship God in repentance and truth? Did the light of eternity illumine his life in the here and now? The death of the counterfeit prophet, Hananiah, came within months.

You may think this passage of Scripture doesn't apply to you. God has not told you that you only have one more year. That's true; your time may be much shorter. You never know. You can be sure your days are numbered by a God in sovereign control. He may have chosen to allot you many more years or only a few more moments. This passage begs you to ask yourself if you are living the kind of life you would want to be living on the day of your death?

I would like to suggest several principles to help you live the life you desire in the light of eternity.

PRINCIPLE 1: LIVE EACH DAY WITH ETERNAL PURPOSE

I was grieved when I heard of Christopher Reeve's accident. The actor, known for his movie portrayal of Superman, fell off of a horse and was paralyzed from his neck down. He can now breathe only with the help of a mechanical respirator. Reeve told Barbara Walters, in an interview, there was a time shortly after the accident when he was so depressed he hoped someone would pull the plug on his respirator. He felt no desire or reason to live— that is, until his wife brought his children for a visit. "Just to be able to see them grow up was worth my living," said Reeve. He was just glad he was alive.

Parents can understand Reeve's sentiments. In the face of hopelessness, he found a purpose for living in his desire to be a part of his children's lives. What do you see as your purpose in life? More importantly, you should ask yourself, *What is God's purpose for my life?*

First, God has *certain expectations* for your life. In the Parable of the Fig Tree, Jesus compares the owner of a vineyard with God. "'A man had a fig tree, planted in his vineyard, and he went to look for fruit on it, but did not find any'" (Luke 13:6). As the man examined his fig tree expecting to find fruit, God examines our lives with the expectation of its fruitfulness.

When Jesus walked on the earth, the fig tree was the most valuable of all trees. It bore crops three times a year. There would be fruit on its branches for ten months of the year. April and May were the only two months it bore no figs. Normally, a young fig tree did not bear fruit for the first three years. It was expected to be fruitful after that.

Like the fig tree planted for its fruit, God created us with a purpose in life. "Whoever trusts in his riches will fall, but the righteous will thrive like a green leaf. He who brings trouble on his family will inherit only wind, and the fool will be servant to the wise. The fruit of the righteous is a tree of life, and he who wins souls is wise" (Prov. 11:28–30). We often confuse purpose in life with professions or possessions. Our purpose is to yield fruit that shows our thankfulness (see Ps. 116:12–13), helps draw others to Christ (see Matt. 5:16), and glorifies God (see Phil. 1:11).

Second, God gives *careful examination* to our lives. "'So [the vineyard owner] said to the man who took care of the vineyard, "For three years now I've been coming to look for fruit on this fig tree and haven't found any. Cut it down! Why should it use up the soil?"'" (Luke 13:7). Like the vineyard owner, God keeps a close watch over our lives. Uselessness and purposelessness invite disaster. We will either self-destruct or face the judgment of God. The owner of the vineyard examined the fruitless tree and determined it should be cut down, so as no longer to deplete the soil of nutrients which could better serve fruitful trees. This is what God did in Hananiah's life. His life was hurting the fruitfulness of the faithful, so God cut him down.

What does God find when He examines your life? The test for you, if you are a Christian, is not what you get out of life, but rather what you put into life. Some say there are three stages of a person's life. When one is young, people say of him, "He will do something great in life." As one grows older, people say of him, "He could do something great if he tried." Toward the end of one's life, people say of him, "He might have done something great if he tried."[1] At what stage of life are you? What do others say of you? Is your life producing fruit? How are you using the gifts and abilities God has given you? What are you doing to further God's kingdom work?

Stephen Covey, in his best-seller *The 7 Habits of Highly Successful People*, recommends to business people who are trying to make sense out of their lives to do the following. Imagine going to your own funeral and listening to four people speak about your life. The first person would be a member of your family, the second speaker would be a friend, the third would be a business associate, and the fourth would be someone from your church. The question is, assuming that they were completely honest, what would you like them to say? What kind of father or mother do you want to be; what kind of friend, coworker, or church member?[2]

How will we be remembered and eulogized? That's a sobering thought. While it is interesting, and perhaps highly motivating, to think of living our lives to be the kind of person others would love and admire, that should not be the primary purpose for a believer. Our will should be to do the will of God and to please God. We must value what God thinks of us more highly than what others think of us. When we stand before God, what kind of eulogy will He deliver for us? Another point must be made. Like, Hananiah we may be able to fool others into thinking we are someone we are not. We cannot fool God. Only God can judge our lives (see Rom. 2:16), and He will.

Third, while God is judge and just, He is also gracious in His *compassionate extension* of mercy to those who humbly seek His favor. In the Parable of the Fig Tree, the vineyard worker asks the owner to ""leave [the fig tree] alone for one more year, and I'll dig around it and fertilize it. If it bears fruit next year, fine! If not, then cut it down"" (Luke 13:8–9). The fig tree had an ally who advocated another year for the tree to have an opportunity to bear fruit. The ally pledged his intercessory help in grooming the tree for productivity. The tree was given one more year to produce fruit.

We're given no indication that Hananiah had an ally. He was told his time was limited to a year or less; yet, there's no evidence he heeded Jeremiah's warning or sought Jeremiah's help. As we think about these two passages, it is important to recognize Jesus as the ally of sinners who on their own bear no fruit, sinners whose days are numbered. Without His intercession, sacrificing Himself on their behalf, they would be judged unworthy of God's favor. We are also forced, as we look at these passages, to ask the question: Will we, as sinners, respond as Hananiah or will we take advantage of the time afforded us to seek salvation in order to bear fruit? Will we live each day with the purpose of glorifying the Father through the fruit we bear?

PRINCIPLE 2: INVEST EACH DAY IN ETERNAL TREASURES

As the fig tree belongs to the owner of the vineyard, our lives do indeed belong to God. He owns not only our possessions and our bodies, but also the very breath of life in us. The life we have in this earthly body is on loan from God for a short time. It's borrowed time, and when that time gets extended, we call it "a new lease on life." With the realization that our lives are not our own, our time is not our own, and our possessions are not our own, we have little about which to boast—except Jesus Christ.

> God chose the foolish things of the world to shame the wise; God chose the weak things of the world to shame the strong. He chose the lowly things of this world and the despised things—and the things that are not—to nullify the things that are, so that no one may boast before him. It is because of him that you are in Christ Jesus, who has become for us wisdom from God—that is, our righteousness, holiness

191

and redemption. Therefore, as it is written: "Let him who boasts boast in the Lord." (1 Cor. 1:27–31)

Living in the light of eternity should humble us. Showing off how much treasure we have stored up for ourselves should no longer seem important to us. There are those, however, who hoard their wealth and count their money over and over, as if their treasures had some eternal value, as if they could take it with them, or as if they were unaware their days are numbered. It is all a matter of having an eternal perspective. When we truly begin to comprehend all that Christ has purchased for us, our acquisitions seem as nothing. Jesus said, "'For where your treasure is, there your heart will be also'" (Luke 12:34).

Perhaps you have heard the story of the rich old man who was determined no one else would get all his money when he died. He made his wife promise to bury it all with him. He was worth about $10 million. At first the man's wife thought he was crazy and would not agree to do it. Finally, after much persistence, the old man convinced her to do it.

On his death bed the old man's last words to his wife were, "Remember, you promised I could keep all my money." As everyone was leaving the grave site, just before the casket was closed, his wife stood there alone to pay her last respects. She took out a check for $10 million and slyly hid it in her husband's coat pocket. "There, you have it," she said curtly. "Take it with you and cash it any time you choose!"

Many people live as though they think they can take it with them. Two men came to Jesus with a dispute over how to divide their family inheritance. He told them a parable about a rich man who had more wealth than he could manage. To handle the abundance, the man built bigger barns, tearing down the smaller ones, so that he could store up more riches. "'But God said to him, "You fool! This very night your life will be demanded from you. Then who will get what you have prepared for yourself?"'" Jesus added, "'This is how it will be with anyone who stores up things for himself but is not rich toward God'" (Luke 12:20–21).

How can we be rich toward God? Paul, in encouraging believers in Corinth to be generous toward others, exhorted them: "Just as you excel in everything—in faith, in speech, in knowledge, in complete earnestness and in your love for us—see that you also excel in this grace of giving. . . . I want to test the sincerity of your love . . . . For you know the grace of our Lord Jesus Christ, that though he was rich, yet for your sakes he became poor, so that you through his poverty might become rich" (2 Cor. 8:7–9).

Paul gives us a way to be eternally rich toward God. It is by living a self-sacrificial life of serving and giving to others as Jesus Christ did while on earth. "'Do not store up for yourselves treasures on earth, where moth and rust destroy, and where thieves break in and steal. But store up for yourselves treasures in heaven, where moth and rust do not destroy, and where thieves do not break in and steal'" (Matt. 6:19–20).

What are those treasures? They are heavenly rewards awaiting us, as Christians, in heaven. When we get to heaven, we are probably going to be shocked by many things. One thing that may take us by surprise is the way God chooses to reward even the smallest act of kindness done in the name of the Lord. Imagine what God, who created the world in six days, has done in the two thousand years since He said He was going to prepare a place for us! I would not be surprised to find that for a single act of faith and obedience, the eternal reward will far outweigh all the collected wealth of this present world. This reward will be a treasure which is both eternal and imperishable. The Bible says, "No eye has seen, no ear has heard, no mind has conceived what God has prepared for those who love him" (1 Cor. 2.9).

How then do we attain those treasures which are eternal? This leads us to the next principle.

PRINCIPLE 3: PRIORITIZE EACH DAY FOR MAXIMUM ETERNAL BENEFIT

Management is the art of getting a job done effectively and efficiently. Leadership is the art of deciding what ought to be done. Some people are so busy managing their lives, they never get around to the issue of personal leadership. What ought they be doing? What should be tops on their lists of priorities?

Living in the light of eternity is an act of faith that translates into everyday attitudes and actions—values and priorities. We should let our lives be driven only by the goals and priorities which will be significant when our lives are over. Those goals and priorities, based on eternal values, should become our definition of success.

In December of 1994, I went to Atlanta to meet with the Order of Business Committee of the Southern Baptist Convention. One of the purposes of the meeting was to walk through the Georgia Dome, the sight of our upcoming convention. After walking through the entire facility, I was led out onto the field. I've watched a number of football games televised from this very field. As I walked along the twenty-yard line, I forgot, for a moment, all about the Southern Baptist Convention. I began to relive a youthful fantasy.

There were ten seconds left in the game. I imagined myself taking the hand-off, breaking through the line, juking to the right, spinning to the left, putting my head down, and diving for the goal line—*touchdown!* The game was over and we had won! The crowd went wild! I spiked the ball and did a Baptist boogaloo in the end-zone. The entire team cleared the bench, knocked me down, and piled on top of me under the goal. The fans began pouring out of the stands onto the field while the announcer kept screaming into the microphone, *"Henry scores! The Packers win!"*

I was abruptly brought back to reality when one of the committee members grabbed my arm and directed me to the side of the field. It was easy for me, in those few moments, to forget the Convention and focus on a dream common to many: to be a successful and adored sports hero. Reality for me, however, was a plan of God much different from being a football hero. Doing the will of God has been my number-one priority—even if it means not getting my picture on the cover of *Sports Illustrated.* Heaven—not a pro game or even a Southern Baptist Convention—will be my Super Bowl.

SEEK FIRST GOD'S KINGDOM

If we do not have clearly defined priorities, we will wind up simply reacting to the temporal goals and values of others around us. There are a lot of people out there who are glad to enlist us in their system of values and beliefs. If we don't allow God to help us plot our own courses, we may wind up following someone else's course by default. What then should be our method of determining God's priorities for our lives? "Then Jesus said to his disciples: 'Therefore I tell you, do not worry about your life, what you will eat; or about your body, what you will wear. Life is more than food, and the body more than clothes. . . . For the pagan world runs after all such things, and your Father knows that you need them. But seek his kingdom, and these things will be given to you as well'" (Luke 12:22–23, 30–31).

God has set seeking His eternal kingdom as our first priority. We should seek to know Him and to love Him, to serve Him and

194

to worship Him above and beyond all other pursuits. A popular "formula" for Christian prioritization is God, family, church, job, others, and recreation. This is antithetical to the world's value system. Our priorities will reflect our kingdom perspective—good or bad, godly or worldly.

Living with an eye on eternity will bring our lives into proper focus. Eternity is primary. Heaven must be our ultimate goal. The matter of proper perspective is a matter of keeping our sights set on God's kingdom while most everything in the world seeks to distract us and distort our vision.

True, we live in the present, but there must be that sense of the *not yet*. The consummation of the redemption process through Jesus Christ comes only in His kingdom. Finding peace and joy in all circumstances is gained only by our attaining this eternal perspective. "So we fix our eyes not on what is seen, but what is unseen. For what is seen is temporary, but what is unseen is eternal" (2 Cor. 4:18). Only when we are able to view this world in the light of the world to come will we be able to see life, at least in part, as God sees it. This is how we keep life in perspective.

NOTES

CHAPTER 1

1. "A Telescope Built by Mr. Magoo," *U.S. News & World Report* (9 July 1990), 14.
2. Jeffrey R. M. Kunz, ed., *The American Medical Association Family Medical Guide* (New York: Random House, 1982), 311.
3. Walter L. Walker, "Zinger," *New Man Magazine* (May–June 1994), 20–23.
4. Larry Crabb, *Inside Out* (Colorado Springs: NavPress, 1988), 55–56.

CHAPTER 2

1. James W. Michaels, "Oh, Our Aching Angst," *Forbes* (14 September 1992): 47–78.
2. Ronald Grover, Joseph Weber, Richard Melcher, "The Entertainment Economy," *Business Week* (14 March 1994): 59.
3. Gene Edwards, *A Tale of Three Kings* (Augusta, Maine: Christian Books, 1980), 19–23.

CHAPTER 3

1. Robert Hemfelt, Frank Minirth, and Paul Meier, *We Are Driven* (Nashville: Thomas Nelson, 1991), 16–17.
2. Ibid., 237.

CHAPTER 4

1. Larry Burkett, *Whatever Happened to the American Dream* (Chicago: Moody Press, 1993), 27.
2. Don Richardson, *Eternity in Their Hearts* (Ventura, Calif.: Regal Books, 1981), n.p.

197

CHAPTER 5

1. J. Dwight Pentecost, *Man's Problems—God's Answers* (Chicago: Moody Press, 1972), 13.

2. Earl D. Wilson, *Counseling and Guilt* (Dallas: Word Publishing, 1987), 71.

3. Ed Young, *From Bad Beginnings to Happy Endings* (Nashville: Thomas Nelson, 1994), 163.

4. Paul Faulkner, *Making Things Right, When Things Go Wrong* (Fort Worth: Sweet Publishing, 1986), 101.

5. Ibid., 103.

6. David A. Seamands, *Healing for Damaged Emotions* (Wheaton, Ill.: Victor Books, 1985), 28.

7. Joel C. Gregory, *Growing Pains of the Soul* (Waco, Tex.: Word Books, 1987), 48.

8. Ibid., 49.

9. Lawrence Crabb, *Effective Biblical Counseling* (Grand Rapids, Mich.: Zondervan, 1977), 160.

10. Fanny J. Crosby, "Blessed Assurance, Jesus Is Mine," 1820–1915.

CHAPTER 6

1. David A. Seamands, *Healing Grace* (Wheaton, Ill.: Victor Books, 1988), 200–201.

2. F. W. Farrat, "The Camel and the Needle's Eye," *The Expositor* (1876): 369–80.

3. Josephus, *The Antiquities of the Jews,* book 8, 15.5 published in *The Works of Josephus* (Peabody, Mass.: Hendrickson, 1987), 243.

4. Alexander Whyte, *Bible Characters* (Grand Rapids, Mich.: Zondervan, 1974), 373.

5. William Cooper, "There Is a Fountain," 1731–1800.

6. Dietrich Bonhoeffer, *The Cost of Discipleship,* trans. R. H. Fuller (New York: MacMillan, 1966), 45.

CHAPTER 7

1. James Patterson, *The Day America Told the Truth* (New York: Prentice Hall, 1991), 66.

2. *Reader's Digest,* March 1995, 169.

3. R. Kent Hughes, *Disciplines of a Godly Man* (Wheaton, Ill.: Crossway Books, 1991), 121.

4. *The Mission Statement,* The First Academy, 2667 Bruton Blvd., Orlando, Fla., 32805.

5. Ibid., 45.

6. Doug Sherman and William Hendricks, *Keeping Your Ethical Edge Sharp* (Colorado Springs, Colo.: NavPress, 1990), 25.

7. Randel Everett, *Pillars* (Pensacola, Fla.: Ardara House, 1994), 102.

8. Sinclair B. Ferguson, *The Communicator's Commentary: Daniel* (Waco, Tex.: Word Books, 1988), 34–36.

9. Victor E. Frankl, *Man's Search for Meaning* (New York: Pocket Books, 1959), 104.

10. Hans Christian Anderson, "The Emperor's New Clothes," in *The Book of Virtues,* William J. Bennett, ed. (New York: Simon & Schuster, 1993), 630–34.

CHAPTER 8

1. William Raspberry, "Why the American Family Is in Trouble," *Orlando Sentinel Star* (3 June 1978).
2. George Barna, *The Future of the American Family* (Chicago: Moody Press, 1993), 23.
3. Ibid., 93.
4. Russell Chandler, *Racing Toward 2001: The Forces Shaping America's Religious Future* (Grand Rapids: Zondervan; San Francisco: Harper, 1992), 90.
5. Nick Stinnett, *Family Building* (Ventura, Calif.: Regal Books, 1985), 38.
6. Robert A. Schuller, *Robert Schuller's Life Changers* (Old Tappan, N.J.: Fleming H. Revell Co., 1981), 67–68.
7. Alan Mawhinney, "Family of God" lectures, Reformed Theological Seminary, Orlando, Fla., Spring 1992.
8. Romans 8:15–23; 9:1–4; Galatians 4:4–7; Ephesians 1:3–14.
9. Dan Clark, "Weathering the Storm," in *Chicken Soup for the Soul*, Jack Canfield and Mark Victor Hansen (Deerfield Beach, Fla.: Health Communications, 1993), 65–66.

CHAPTER 9

1. Bob Buford, *Half Time* (Grand Rapids: Zondervan, 1994), 20.
2. Tim Kimmel, "Grooming Your Pallbearers," in *What Makes a Man*, Bill McCartney, (Colorado Springs: NavPress, 1992), 134–35.
3. Alan Loy McGinnis, *The Friendship Factor* (Minneapolis: Augsburg, 1979), 11.
4. Ibid.
5. Ibid.

CHAPTER 10

1. David Ring, *Just as I Am* (Chicago: Moody Press, 1993), 22–23.
2. Ibid., 38–39.
3. John R. Stott, *Baptism and Fullness: The Work of the Holy Spirit Today* (Downers Grove, Ill.: InterVarsity Press, n.d.), 57.

CHAPTER 11

1. Mark Victor Hansen, *Chicken Soup for the Soul* (Deerfield Beach, Fla.: Health Communications, 1993), 256–58.
2. B. Clayton Bell, pastor of Highland Park Presbyterian Church, Dallas, Texas.
3. George Croly, "Spirit of God, Descend upon My Heart," 1854.
4. Richard Wilbur, "Parable," *Oxford Book of Short Poems,* ed. James Michie and P. J. Kavanagh (New York: Oxford University Press, 1985), n.p.

CHAPTER 12

1. Ann Landers, *Chicago Tribune,* 17 September 1989.
2. Charles R. Swindoll, *Living above the Level of Mediocrity* (Waco, Tex.: Word Books, 1987), 98.
3. Doug Murren, *Keeping Your Dreams Alive* (Altamonte Springs, Fla.: Creation House, 1993), 75.
4. Ibid., 77.
5. J. Dwight Pentecost, *Man's Problems, God's Answers* (Chicago: Moody Press, 1972), 43.

6. Walter Elliott, *The Spiritual Life* (Paulist Press), "Quotable Quotes," *Reader's Digest*, June 1985.

7. Anne and Ray Ortlund, *You Don't Have to Quit* (Nashville: Oliver-Nelson, 1986), 69–70.

8. Robert H. Schuller, *Tough Times Never Last, But Tough People Do!* (Nashville: Thomas Nelson, 1983), 61.

CHAPTER 13

1. William Barclay, *And Jesus Said* (Philadelphia: The Westminster Press, 1970), 130–31.

2. Stephen R. Covey, *The 7 Habits of Highly Successful People* (New York: Simon and Schuster, 1989), 96–97.